SIMPLY
PSYCHOLOGY

DK LONDON

Project Editor Rose Blackett-Ord
Senior Art Editor Phil Gamble
Editors Andrew Szudek, Kathryn Hill,
Joanna Edwards
US Editor Kayla Dugger
Designer Daksheeta Pattni
Managing Editor Gareth Jones
Senior Managing Art Editor Lee Griffiths
Production Editor Gillian Reid
Senior Production Controller Rachel Ng
Jacket Design Development Manager
Sophia M.T.T.
Jacket Designer Akiko Kato
Associate Publishing Director Liz Wheeler
Art Director Karen Self
Publishing Director Jonathan Metcalf

First American Edition, 2022
Published in the United States by DK Publishing
1745 Broadway, 20th Floor, New York NY 10019

A catalog record for this book
is available from the Library of Congress.
ISBN 978-0-7440-4837-7

Printed and bound in China

For the curious
www.dk.com

This book was made with Forest
Stewardship Council™ certified
paper—one small step in DK's
commitment to a sustainable future.
For more information go to
www.dk.com/our-green-pledge

FSC
www.fsc.org
MIX
Paper from
responsible sources
FSC™ C018179

CONSULTANT
Merrin Lazyan is a radio and podcast producer, content developer, writer, and editor. She studied psychology at Harvard University and has worked on several books spanning a broad range of topics.

CONTRIBUTORS
Steve Parker holds a First Class Honours degree in Zoology and is a Senior Scientific Fellow of the Zoological Society. He has written extensively on human biology, especially on the brain's role in instincts, emotions, and learning, and other aspects of behavior.

Nancy Sachar Sidhu is a clinical psychologist in Chester, New Jersey, with degrees from the University of Pennsylvania and California School of Professional Psychology. She has a private practice treating children, teenagers, and adults.

Andrew Szudek is a writer and editor who studied philosophy at Cambridge University, specializing in the philosophy of mind.

Victoria Uwannah is a counseling psychologist who received her doctorate from Surrey University. She works in private practice, offering therapy for individuals and couples.

Marcus Weeks studied music and philosophy in college and worked as a teacher, piano restorer, and musician before embarking on a career as a writer. He has authored and contributed to numerous books on philosophy, psychology, and the arts.

CONTENTS

7   **INTRODUCTION**

STUDYING
THE **MIND**

10   **MIND AND BODY**
     Dualism

11   **ONLY MATTER**
     Physicalism

12   **INTERNAL DIVISIONS**
     The tripartite soul

13   **NATURE OR NURTURE?**
     Heredity

14   **EMOTIONAL EXCESS**
     Hysteria

15   **PATTERNS IN COMMON**
     Defining mental disorders

16   **LOOKING WITHIN**
     Introspection

17   **THREE ELEMENTS**
     Structuralism

18   **STUDYING THE WHOLE**
     Gestalt psychology

19   **THE FORGETTING CURVE**
     Learned information

20   **ADAPTING TO THE WORLD**
     Functionalism

21   **THE EMOTIONAL MIND**
     *The James–Lange theory
     of emotion*

22   **DISSECTING THE MIND**
     Psychoanalytic theory

24   **BRINGING UP THE PAST**
     Psychoanalysis

25   **SHIELDING THE EGO**
     Defense mechanisms

26   **NEVER GOOD ENOUGH**
     Inferiority complex

27   **WHAT DO YOU SEE?**
     Rorschach tests

28   **THE SHARED MIND**
     The collective unconscious

29   **SEEKING COMPLETENESS**
     Register theory

30   **DISCOVERING OTHERS**
     Object relations theory

31   **BECOMING ONESELF**
     Self-realization

32   **PAVLOVIAN RESPONSES**
     Classical conditioning

33   **THE "LITTLE ALBERT"
     EXPERIMENT**
     Behavioral conditioning

34   **REPEAT WHEN SATISFIED**
     Law of effect

35   **SHAPING BEHAVIOR**
     Operant conditioning

36   **COGNITIVE MAPS**
     Latent learning

37   **BRIDGING THE GAP**
     Cognitive behaviorism

38   **THE HIERARCHY OF NEEDS**
     Self-actualization

39   **COMPLETE SUPPORT AND
     ACCEPTANCE**
     Unconditional positive regard

40   **THE SCIENCE OF HAPPINESS**
     Positive psychology

41   **THE MIND EVOLVED**
     Evolutionary psychology

42   **BIOLOGICAL BEHAVIOR**
     Biopsychology

GROWTH AND DEVELOPMENT

46 **ORGANIZING IDEAS**
Schemas

47 **HOW CHILDREN THINK**
The four stages of development

48 **A NATURAL PROCESS**
Child-centered learning

49 **LEARNING TOGETHER**
Social constructivism

50 **THE EIGHT STAGES OF HUMAN LIFE**
Psychosocial development

52 **INSTINCTIVE BEHAVIOR**
Fixed-action patterns

53 **COPYING OTHERS**
Social learning theory

54 **EARLY RELATIONSHIPS**
Attachment theory

55 **LONGING FOR COMFORT**
Infant development

56 **FEELING SECURE**
The Strange Situation

57 **RESPONSES TO ABUSE**
Genetics and development

58 **BORN TO SPEAK**
Language development

59 **RIGHT OR WRONG?**
Moral development

60 **THE DOLL TESTS**
Race and self-esteem

61 **REDUCING PREJUDICE**
Jigsaw Classrooms

62 **EXPLORING ETHNICITY**
Ethnic and racial identity development

63 **BOY OR GIRL?**
Gender development

64 **GENDER STEREOTYPES**
Sex differences

65 **DIFFERENT KINDS OF BRAINS?**
Autism, sex, and gender

SELF AND SOCIETY

68 **SOCIAL ANIMALS**
Cultural naturalism

69 **THE LIFE SPACE**
Field theory

70 **RESEARCHING SEXUALITY**
Psychology of sex

71 **SEVEN KINDS OF LOVE**
Triangular theory of love

72 **MAJORITY RULES**
Social conformity

73 **AUTHORITY FIGURES**
Obedience

74 **THE PERCEPTION OF POWER**
The Stanford prison experiment

75 **CONTEXT MATTERS**
Aronson's First Law

76 **COMPETING FOR RESOURCES**
Realistic conflict theory

77 **AVOIDING RESPONSIBILITY**
The bystander effect

78 **PREFERRING THE FAMILIAR**
Mere-exposure effect

79 **THEIR JUST DESERTS?**
The "just-world" hypothesis

80 **MAKING ASSUMPTIONS**
Prejudice

81 **MEASURING OPINIONS**
*The Attitudes Toward
Women Scale*

82 **STUDYING ORGANIZATIONS**
Organizational psychology

84 **EXAMINING OPPRESSION**
Liberation psychology

85 **FREE TO CHOOSE**
Choice theory

102 **FAST AND SLOW DECISIONS**
Heuristics

103 **JUMPING TO CONCLUSIONS**
Cognitive bias

104 **SPIRITUAL EXERCISE**
Mindfulness and meditation

105 **IN THE ZONE**
Flow

THOUGHTS
AND **PROCESSES**

DISORDERS AND
THERAPIES

88 **THE CONSCIOUS MIND**
Consciousness

90 **PROCESSING SENSATIONS**
Perception

92 **IDENTIFYING OBJECTS**
Pattern recognition

93 **BASIC FEELINGS**
Psychology of emotions

94 **MAGIC NUMBER SEVEN**
Information processing

95 **A BIOLOGICAL COMPUTER**
Computational theory of mind

96 **FOCUSING ATTENTION**
Attention theory

97 **STRIVING FOR CONSISTENCY**
Cognitive dissonance

98 **STORAGE STRUCTURE**
Long-term memory

99 **REWRITING THE PAST**
False memory

100 **MEMORY MALFUNCTION**
The seven sins of memory

108 **DIAGNOSING DISORDERS**
Psychiatric classification systems

110 **PROCESSING DIFFERENTLY**
Autism spectrum disorder

111 **HARD TO FOCUS**
*Attention deficit hyperactivity
disorder*

112 **DELUSIONS, PARANOIA, AND
ALTERED THINKING**
Schizophrenia

113 **EXTREME HIGHS AND LOWS**
Bipolar disorder

114 **A DARK CLOUD**
Depression

115 **PREGNANCY, PARENTHOOD,
AND MENTAL HEALTH**
Perinatal mental illness

116 **FEARING THE WORST**
*Generalized anxiety and
panic disorders*

117 **DEBILITATING FEAR**
Phobias

118 **INTRUSIVE THOUGHTS AND
REPETITIVE URGES**
Obsessive compulsive disorder

119 **DISTORTED SELF-IMAGE**
Body dysmorphic disorder

120 **AFTERMATH OF TRAUMA**
Posttraumatic stress disorder

121 **FRAGMENTED IDENTITY**
Dissociative identity disorder

122 **PROBLEMS WITH EATING**
Eating disorders

123 **STRUGGLING TO RESIST**
Addiction

124 **RELATING DIFFERENTLY**
Personality disorders

126 **TREATING DISORDERS**
Psychological therapies

128 **UNCOVERING THE PAST**
Psychodynamic therapy

129 **BALANCING THE SOUL**
Jungian therapy

130 **PARENT, ADULT, CHILD**
Transactional analysis

131 **LED BY THE CLIENT**
Person-centered therapy

132 **THE WHOLE PERSON**
Gestalt therapy

133 **CONFRONTING EXISTENCE**
Existential therapy

134 **HEALING REASON**
Rational emotive behavior therapy

135 **CHANGING PATTERNS**
Cognitive behavioral therapy

136 **GROUP DYNAMICS**
Family systems therapy

137 **FACING TRAUMA**
Eye movement desensitization and reprocessing

138 **TREATING THE BODY**
Medication

139 **NATURAL REACTIONS**
Antipsychiatry

IDENTITY AND DIFFERENCE

142 **HUMAN CHARACTERISTICS**
Trait theory

143 **THE BIG FIVE**
The OCEAN model

144 **ENERGY SOURCES**
Introversion and extroversion

145 **TESTING PERSONALITY**
Personality psychometrics

146 **FLUID AND CRYSTALLIZED**
The Cattell–Horn theory of intelligence

147 **THREE INTELLIGENCES**
Triarchic theory of intelligence

148 **MEASURING CREATIVITY**
The Torrance Tests of Creative Thinking

149 **DRIVING MOTIVATORS**
Need theory

150 **WHO AM I?**
Identity formation

151 **FINDING AN IDENTITY**
Identity status theory

152 **MALE BIAS**
Feminist psychology

153 **AFROCENTRIC PSYCHOLOGY**
Optimal psychology

154 **MINDS AND CULTURES**
Multicultural psychology

156 **INDEX**

WHAT IS PSYCHOLOGY?

Psychology can be described as the scientific study of the mind and human behavior, but that hardly does the subject justice. We humans have been fascinated by the way our minds work and why we behave the way we do since the time of the ancient Greek philosophers. In fact, the term "psychology" originates from their word *psyche*, meaning both "soul" and "mind."

Until comparatively recently, the study of minds was a branch of philosophy. Psychology only became recognized as a science toward the end of the 19th century, when experimental psychologists found ways of applying scientific methods to their research. This new science developed at roughly the same time as advances in physiology and neuroscience, which provided explanations of how our brains and nervous systems work. Psychology bridged the gap between these physical explanations and various philosophers' theories about the mind.

As psychology developed further, it began to share ground with even more disciplines, including the social sciences, medicine, and education. Different branches of psychology emerged, each dealing with different aspects of the subject, such as developmental psychology (see pp.44–65), social psychology (see pp.66–85), and the psychology of difference (see pp.140–155). Other branches dealt specifically with diagnosing and treating psychological disorders (see pp.106–139). More recently, especially with the benefit of brain-imaging technology, it has become possible to study mental processes, and states such as consciousness, which researchers had previously considered to be beyond the scope of scientific study.

Psychology has provided the world with theories and discoveries that help explain what makes human beings tick. Its practical applications have changed our lives, and in particular how society regards mental health. Our curiosity about ourselves is apparently insatiable, and psychology continues to produce fresh insights into our minds and our behavior.

STUDY THE MIND

I N G

In the 19th century, psychologists began to use the scientific method (performing controlled, repeatable experiments) to shed light on the workings of the human mind. Some focused on the nature of experience (how we perceive and think about the world), while others, known as "behaviorists," studied behavior (how we interact with the world). A third group developed "psychoanalytic theory," which proposed that many of our thoughts and behaviors are influenced by unconscious drives and emotions. Later, "humanist" psychologists argued that each of us is unique and can only be understood in terms of our own subjective experience.

MIND AND BODY

Throughout history, most societies have distinguished between the physical body and the mind. In ancient Greece, the philosopher Plato argued that the "psyche," or mind, is connected to the "eternal realm of the Forms": a world that we cannot perceive with our senses, but from which we derive all of our ideas about reality. Known as dualism, this idea that the mind is separate from the body was defended by the 17th-century philosopher René Descartes, and is still popular today.

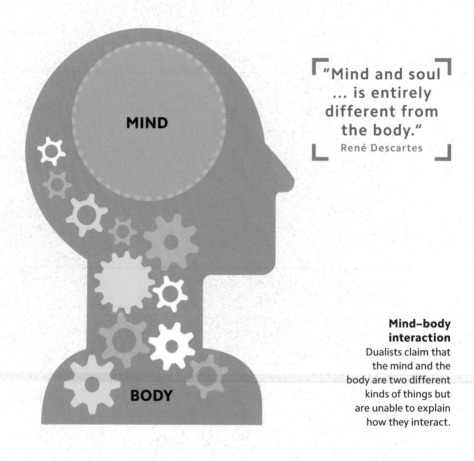

MIND

BODY

"Mind and soul
... is entirely
different from
the body."
René Descartes

**Mind–body
interaction**
Dualists claim that
the mind and the
body are two different
kinds of things but
are unable to explain
how they interact.

ONLY MATTER

The first scientists were the philosophers of ancient Greece. Many of them were dualists (see opposite), but some believed that the only thing that exists is physical matter. Democritus, for example, claimed that the psyche is composed of physical particles called "fire atoms," which bring inanimate matter to life. Known as physicalism, this idea was reformulated by the 17th-century philosopher Thomas Hobbes, who argued that the mind is nothing but the brain in action.

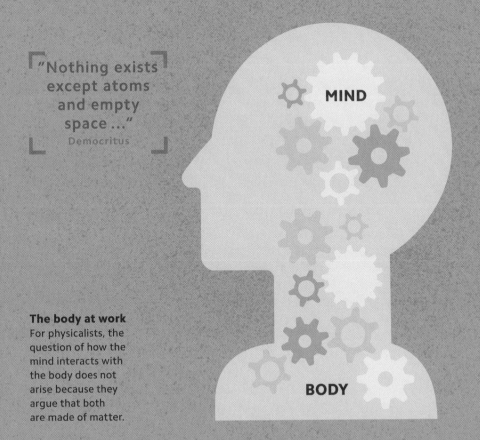

"Nothing exists except atoms and empty space ..."
Democritus

The body at work
For physicalists, the question of how the mind interacts with the body does not arise because they argue that both are made of matter.

MIND

BODY

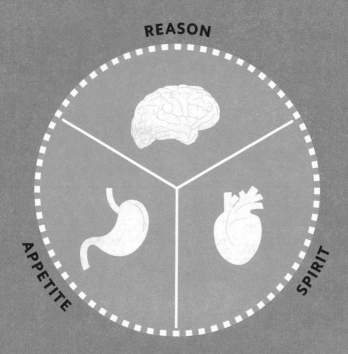

Sources of the soul
Plato associated reason, spirit,
and appetite (the three parts of
the "soul") with the brain, heart,
and stomach, respectively.

REASON

APPETITE

SPIRIT

INTERNAL DIVISIONS

In the *Republic*, Plato (see p.10) divided the "soul," or mind, into
three parts: reason, spirit, and appetite. Reason gives us the ability
to think and to make sound judgments. Spirit is our life force and
enables us to act with courage. Appetite is desire, which we keep in
check by using reason. For Plato, a healthy person keeps all three
elements in balance. Over 2,000 years later, Sigmund Freud
divided the mind into three similar categories (see p.22).

NATURE OR NURTURE?

In 1875, Francis Galton coined the phrase "nature versus nurture." "Nature" refers to the genetically determined traits that we inherit from our biological parents. "Nurture" refers to our upbringing, environment, and life experiences. Galton investigated how these two kinds of influence shape our personalities by studying twins who had almost identical genes but who grew up in different environments. Some of his conclusions are now thought to be deeply problematic, and researchers still debate whether nature or nurture has the greater influence on our development.

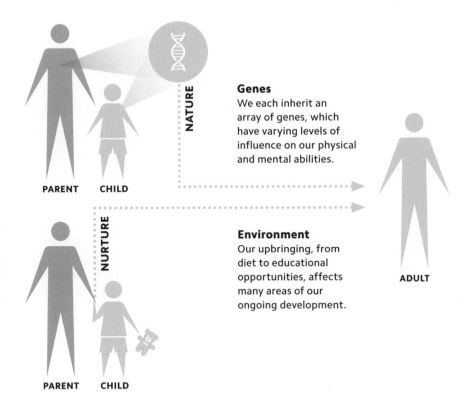

NATURE

PARENT   CHILD

Genes
We each inherit an array of genes, which have varying levels of influence on our physical and mental abilities.

NURTURE

PARENT   CHILD

Environment
Our upbringing, from diet to educational opportunities, affects many areas of our ongoing development.

ADULT

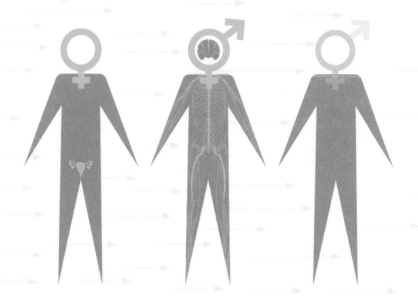

Biological

Until the 19th century, people believed that "hysteria," from the Greek *hystera* (uterus), originated in the womb, affecting only women.

Neurological

Charcot made advances in understanding the nervous system and thought that mental disorders resulted from neurological problems.

Psychological

Freud claimed that mental disorders have psychological rather than physical causes— but he still linked them to sexuality and gender.

EMOTIONAL EXCESS

Some of the earliest clinical diagnoses of mental disorders were made by ancient Egyptian and Greek physicians. They believed that certain abnormal emotional or behavioral conditions were particular to women, attributing them to problems of the uterus. Alternative explanations emerged during the 19th century with the work of neurologists such as Jean-Martin Charcot. However, in the late 19th century, Sigmund Freud (see p.22) proposed that the mental disorders then collectively known as "hysteria" were in fact psychological, rather than physical, in origin. His theories revolutionized the treatment of such conditions.

In the 18th and early 19th centuries, doctors described mental illnesses using broad terms such as "hysteria" (see opposite) or "insanity." Early psychiatrists sought to develop a more nuanced classification system, identifying many conditions by their symptoms. Then in 1899, Emil Kraepelin suggested a new way of defining and classifying mental illnesses: by grouping them according to common patterns of symptoms noted over time, not just by individual symptoms alone.

SHARED SYMPTOMS

Kraepelin divided mental illnesses into two main classes: "dementia praecox" (later labeled "schizophrenia") and "manic depression" (including what is now called "bipolar disorder," as well as other emotional disorders). These classes of disorder often have symptoms in common, but Kraepelin recognized that each one also has its own distinctive pattern of symptoms. His work had a major influence on 20th-century methods for defining mental disorders.

"MANIC DEPRESSION"

PATTERNS IN COMMON

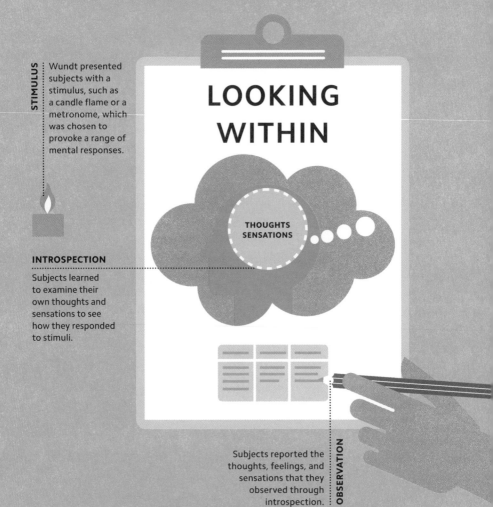

Wundt presented subjects with a stimulus, such as a candle flame or a metronome, which was chosen to provoke a range of mental responses.

LOOKING WITHIN

**THOUGHTS
SENSATIONS**

INTROSPECTION

Subjects learned to examine their own thoughts and sensations to see how they responded to stimuli.

Subjects reported the thoughts, feelings, and sensations that they observed through introspection.

OBSERVATION

In 1879, Wilhelm Wundt set up the first experimental psychology laboratory. In it, he attempted to analyze the workings of the human mind. The first problem he had to overcome was the fact that the only mind that anyone has direct access to is their own. Wundt's solution to this was to institute a strict process that he called "introspection," in which volunteers were trained to look into their own minds and accurately report their thoughts, feelings, and sensations, particularly in response to specific stimuli.

THREE ELEMENTS

Continuing Wundt's experimental work on introspection (see opposite), Edward B. Titchener tried to explain how the mind produces conscious experience. In a theory known as "structuralism," he identified three elements of consciousness: sensations, images, and feelings. He argued that these elements are the building blocks of three states of experience: sensations form our perceptions, or "discernments"; images form our thoughts; and feelings form our emotions. Working together, they form the structure of conscious experience.

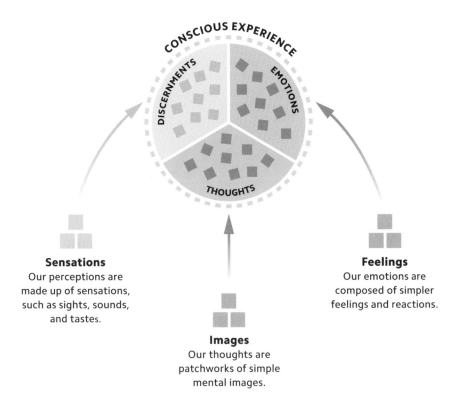

Sensations
Our perceptions are made up of sensations, such as sights, sounds, and tastes.

Images
Our thoughts are patchworks of simple mental images.

Feelings
Our emotions are composed of simpler feelings and reactions.

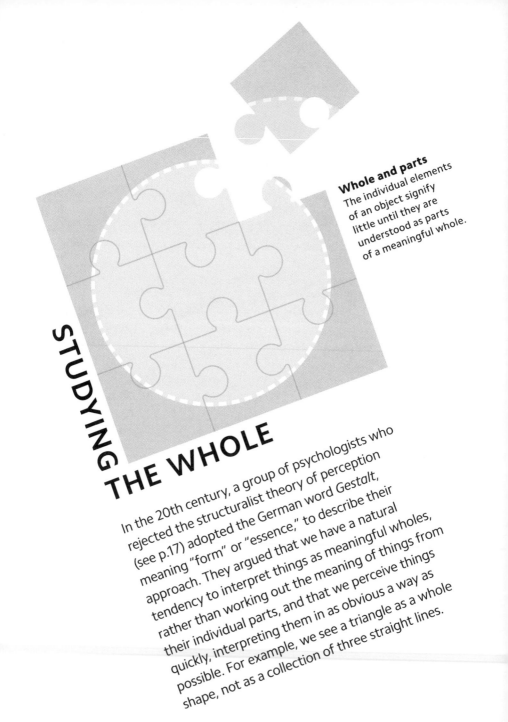

Whole and parts
The individual elements of an object signify little until they are understood as parts of a meaningful whole.

STUDYING THE WHOLE

In the 20th century, a group of psychologists who rejected the structuralist theory of perception (see p.17) adopted the German word *Gestalt*, meaning "form" or "essence," to describe their approach. They argued that we have a natural tendency to interpret things as meaningful wholes, rather than working out the meaning of things from their individual parts, and that we perceive things quickly, interpreting them in as obvious a way as possible. For example, we see a triangle as a whole shape, not as a collection of three straight lines.

Hermann Ebbinghaus performed an experiment to test the nature of memory. He familiarized himself with a list of meaningless syllables, such as VUT and LEF, and then periodically tested himself to see how many he could remember. He plotted his results on a graph that is now known as the "forgetting curve." The graph showed that, without rereading the original list, he forgot half of the syllables in a matter of days, after which he forgot most of the others at a slower rate. Ebbinghaus demonstrated that we quickly forget learned information and that, to retain it, we need to return to it daily.

> "Mental events ... are not passive happenings, but the acts of a subject."
> Hermann Ebbinghaus

THE FORGETTING CURVE

Stream of consciousness
Previous thinkers believed that consciousness is composed of different things; James compared it to a stream in which all of the mind's processes are contained.

For James, the function of the stream of consciousness is to enable us to adapt to our environment— for example, by making plans for the future.

FUTURE PLANS

"My thinking is first and last and always for the sake of my doing."
William James

ADAPTING TO THE WORLD

In the late 19th century, some psychologists began to study the mind in terms of what it does rather than what it is. Known as "functionalists," they abandoned the structuralist approach of studying human experience (see p.17) and instead analyzed the function of mental processes. They were influenced by the biologist Charles Darwin, who argued that living things evolve over time as they adapt to changing environments. William James, who pioneered this approach, claimed that thoughts and beliefs help us adapt to the world around us.

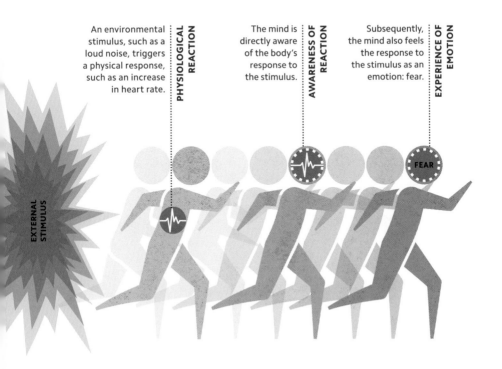

An environmental stimulus, such as a loud noise, triggers a physical response, such as an increase in heart rate.

PHYSIOLOGICAL REACTION

The mind is directly aware of the body's response to the stimulus.

AWARENESS OF REACTION

Subsequently, the mind also feels the response to the stimulus as an emotion: fear.

EXPERIENCE OF EMOTION

EXTERNAL STIMULUS

FEAR

THE EMOTIONAL MIND

Many 19th-century scientists believed that emotions are caused by thoughts. They argued, for example, that when a person hears a loud noise, their feeling of fear is caused by a "cognitive event" in which the mind recognizes danger and triggers the fear emotion. In the mid-1880s, William James (see opposite) and the physician Carl Lange independently overturned this idea. They argued that what we see in the world has a direct physical impact on our bodies and that it is our awareness of those changes that we experience as emotion.

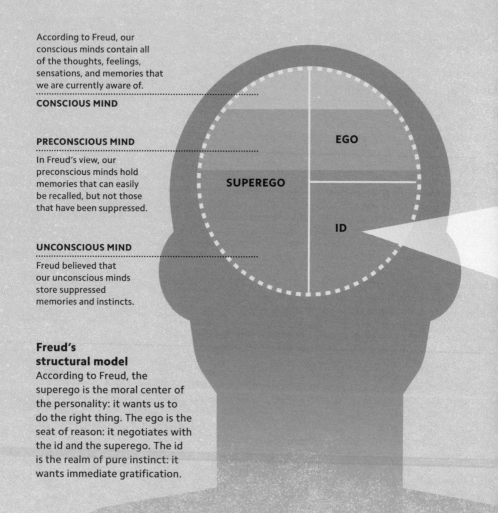

"... the unconscious is the real psychic;
its inner nature is just as unknown to us
as the reality of the external world."
Sigmund Freud

According to Freud, our
conscious minds contain all
of the thoughts, feelings,
sensations, and memories that
we are currently aware of.

CONSCIOUS MIND

PRECONSCIOUS MIND

In Freud's view, our
preconscious minds hold
memories that can easily
be recalled, but not those
that have been suppressed.

UNCONSCIOUS MIND

Freud believed that
our unconscious minds
store suppressed
memories and instincts.

EGO

SUPEREGO

ID

Freud's structural model

According to Freud, the
superego is the moral center of
the personality: it wants us to
do the right thing. The ego is the
seat of reason: it negotiates with
the id and the superego. The id
is the realm of pure instinct: it
wants immediate gratification.

DISSECTING THE MIND

In the early 20th century, Sigmund Freud proposed that each person's mind has three levels of consciousness: the conscious, the preconscious, and the unconscious. He also identified three aspects of personality: the superego, the ego, and the id. Freud suggested that the superego and the ego both have conscious, preconscious, and unconscious elements but that the id is entirely unconscious. He claimed that psychological problems arise as a result of conflict between a person's conscious mind and their unconscious beliefs and desires (see p.24).

THANATOS
DEATH
DRIVE

EROS
LIFE DRIVE

Primitive drives
In Freud's view, the id is the primitive, instinctive core of the personality. Entirely unconscious, it is composed of all of our biological drives, which direct us to meet our basic needs. These drives include our sexual and aggressive instincts, which he called "Eros" (the life drive) and "Thanatos" (the death drive) respectively.

INSIGHT

GAINING INSIGHT
....
The goal of
psychoanalysis is
to bring suppressed
memories into the
conscious mind. This
enables the patient to
face these memories
and see them in a
new light.

CONSCIOUS

PRECONSCIOUS

BRINGING UP
THE PAST

UNCONSCIOUS

Sigmund Freud (see
pp.22–23) proposed that
psychological problems arise
when an individual has a traumatic
experience, usually early in life, and
then "suppresses" the memory of what
happened. He argued that such memories
remain active in the unconscious mind, causing
the person to suffer a range of ailments, including
anxiety and depression. In Freud's view, they could
alleviate these ailments by undergoing a process that he
called "psychoanalysis," in which an "analyst" (therapist)
encourages them to talk about whatever comes to mind. He
claimed that this method, known as free association (see p.128),
enables patients to access and face their suppressed memories,
thoughts, feelings, and dreams.

SHIELDING THE EGO

In the 1930s, Anna Freud, the daughter of Sigmund Freud (see pp.22–24), explored the ways in which our unconscious minds manipulate reality in order to protect us from traumatic events and circumstances. She identified a wide range of such "defense mechanisms," including repression (the burying of painful memories) and rationalization (the justification of unacceptable thoughts and behaviors). She attributed these mechanisms to the ego, which, she argued, defends us from both the drives of the id and the demands of the superego (see pp.22–23).

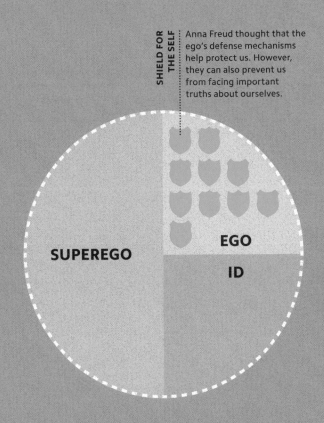

SHIELD FOR THE SELF Anna Freud thought that the ego's defense mechanisms help protect us. However, they can also prevent us from facing important truths about ourselves.

SUPEREGO

EGO

ID

IMAGINED SELF

A person with an inferiority complex may overcompensate for their feelings of inferiority by self-aggrandizing or striving to excel over others.

"A lie would have no sense unless the truth were felt dangerous."

Alfred Adler

An inferiority complex negatively impacts a person's self-esteem and makes them feel inferior to others.

REAL SENSE OF SELF

NEVER GOOD ENOUGH

Alfred Adler coined the term "inferiority complex" to describe a condition in which a person suffers from an overwhelming sense of inferiority that they cannot overcome. He believed that someone with an inferiority complex will often try to overcompensate by, for example, being aggressive or competitive in the company of others in order to hide what they feel is the "truth": that they are inferior. Adler argued that an inferiority complex can impair personality development and may lead to chronic distress if left unchecked.

Hermann Rorschach designed a test that he believed could help diagnose psychological disorders. Under controlled conditions, he showed a series of 10 abstract inkblot pictures to each of his patients and asked them to describe what they saw. Paying close attention to how they reacted to each picture, Rorschach noticed that patients with similar personalities or disorders reacted in similar ways. Where some saw an angry face, for example, others saw a pair of playful bears. Today, some psychologists still use this test to help them assess an individual's personality type.

WHAT DO YOU SEE?

Projecting meaning
The Rorschach test relies on our tendency to project meaning onto abstract patterns. Many people see a downward-facing monster in this inkblot. Other interpretations include animal hide or a skin rug.

Sigmund Freud (see pp.22–24) argued that we each have an unconscious mind that forms symbolic representations of our conscious experiences. Carl Jung, Freud's student, proposed that this personal unconscious is only one part of a collective unconscious mind, which generates "archetypes" (primal imagery common to all human beings). Jung claimed that such imagery can be found not only in our dreams, but also in traditional myths, religions, and fairy tales. Key archetypal images include those of the "Wise Old Man," the "Great Mother," and the "Tree of Life."

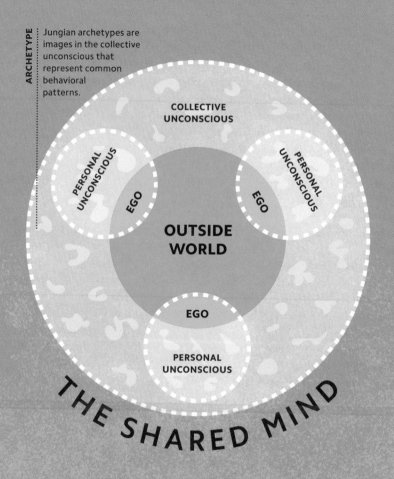

ARCHETYPE Jungian archetypes are images in the collective unconscious that represent common behavioral patterns.

COLLECTIVE UNCONSCIOUS

PERSONAL UNCONSCIOUS

EGO

PERSONAL UNCONSCIOUS

EGO

OUTSIDE WORLD

EGO

PERSONAL UNCONSCIOUS

THE SHARED MIND

SEEKING COMPLETENESS

IMAGINARY

SYMBOLIC

REAL

In the 1950s, Jacques Lacan argued that there are three mutually dependent aspects, or "registers," to "human reality": the "imaginary," the "symbolic," and the "real." The imaginary is the world as it appears to us through our senses. The symbolic is the world as we understand and describe it in language. The real, however, is the world as it is "in itself," which, according to Lacan, we cannot sense, understand, or put into words. He thought that because we can never know the real, we have a constant sense of incompleteness. This sense can either motivate us to do great things or lead us into self-destructive behavior.

DISCOVERING OTHERS

In the 1940s, Melanie Klein argued that very young children do not experience "people" around them, but only "objects" that either delight or frustrate them. A mother's breast, for example, is an object that causes relief, but also resentment when it is taken away. Because an infant does not always get what it wants, it can struggle to understand how the same object can be both "good" and "bad," and so repress its negative feelings toward the bad. According to Klein, healthy infants gradually learn that certain objects are people, and that people are "ambivalent": neither good nor bad, but simply more complicated than they had thought.

"BAD" MOTHER

"GOOD" MOTHER

CHILD

The "unambivalent" world
Klein stated that some children never learn that people are ambivalent: they grow up believing that their mothers are both "good" and "bad." Klein argued that, unable to cope with their conflicting emotions, such infants split their perceptions of their mothers in two.

REAL SELF

"HEALTHY" PERSON

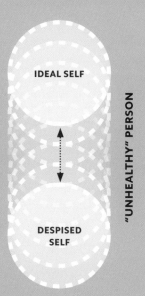

IDEAL SELF

DESPISED SELF

"UNHEALTHY" PERSON

BECOMING ONESELF

Karen Horney believed that many psychological problems are caused by social conditioning rather than biology. In the 1950s, she argued that, under healthy circumstances, people usually have a realistic idea about who they are and what they can achieve. However, due to social pressure, many people have an unrealistic, or idealized, image of who they ought to be. Because this "ideal self" can never be attained, it degenerates into what Horney called the "despised self." The "real self," she argued, is a person's natural self, which has an authentic picture of who they are. Being in touch with this real self is what Horney called "self-realization."

"Pride and self-hate belong inseparably together."
Karen Horney

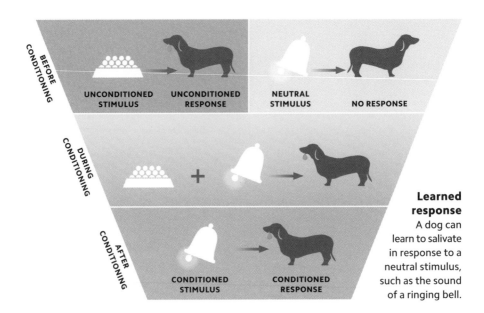

UNCONDITIONED
STIMULUS

UNCONDITIONED
RESPONSE

NEUTRAL
STIMULUS

NO RESPONSE

DURING CONDITIONING

+

AFTER CONDITIONING

**Learned
response**
A dog can
learn to salivate
in response to a
neutral stimulus,
such as the sound
of a ringing bell.

CONDITIONED
STIMULUS

CONDITIONED
RESPONSE

PAVLOVIAN
RESPONSES

In the 1890s, Ivan Pavlov made a discovery
that became the basis of a theory known
as "classical conditioning," which some
psychologists have since applied to humans (see
opposite). Before Pavlov, scientists believed that
animals respond to stimuli in an unconditioned
(instinctive) way—for example, that dogs only salivate
when they are presented with food. However, while
conducting an experiment, Pavlov discovered that dogs also
begin to salivate in response to sounds that they are
conditioned (taught) to associate with being fed. He showed
that animals learn by associating a stimulus with a learned response.

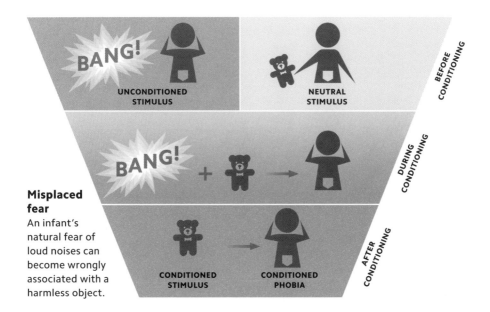

UNCONDITIONED STIMULUS

NEUTRAL STIMULUS

CONDITIONED STIMULUS

CONDITIONED PHOBIA

Misplaced fear
An infant's natural fear of loud noises can become wrongly associated with a harmless object.

THE "LITTLE ALBERT" EXPERIMENT

Ivan Pavlov (see opposite) showed that animals can learn through association. John Watson and Rosalie Rayner argued that the same is true of humans, and in 1919, they decided to prove it. They presented a 9-month-old boy named Albert with a white rat. At first, Albert displayed no fear of the rat. However, two months later, whenever they brought the rat to Albert, Watson banged a hammer on a metal bar, startling the infant. Albert became terrified of the rat and anything that reminded him of it. Even though the rat itself had done nothing to upset the child, Albert's irrational, but conditioned, fear lasted for several months.

REPEAT WHEN SATISFIED

Edward Thorndike believed that animals, including humans, learn new behaviors through a trial-and-error process of responding to their immediate environments. In one experiment, he placed a cat in a box from which the cat could only escape by pressing a lever. To motivate the cat, he placed a fish outside the box. Initially, the cat only got to the fish when it accidentally pushed the lever. However, it soon learned that there was a connection between the lever and the box opening, after which it pressed the lever to get out. Thorndike concluded that animals repeat behavior when it is followed by pleasant consequences. He called this principle the "law of effect."

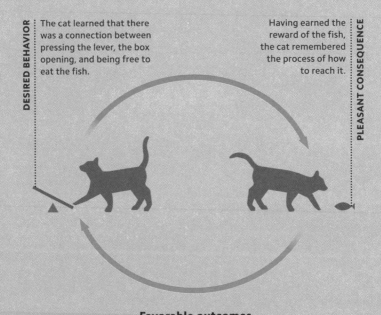

DESIRED BEHAVIOR

The cat learned that there was a connection between pressing the lever, the box opening, and being free to eat the fish.

PLEASANT CONSEQUENCE

Having earned the reward of the fish, the cat remembered the process of how to reach it.

Favorable outcomes
Thorndike's experiment showed that animals repeat actions that lead to favorable outcomes.

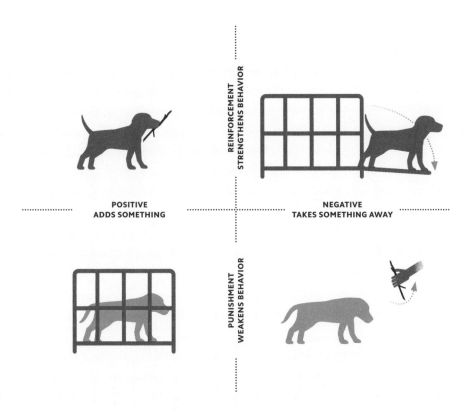

POSITIVE
ADDS SOMETHING

NEGATIVE
TAKES SOMETHING AWAY

REINFORCEMENT
STRENGTHENS BEHAVIOR

PUNISHMENT
WEAKENS BEHAVIOR

SHAPING BEHAVIOR

Building on the work of Edward Thorndike (see opposite),
B. F. Skinner argued that animals and humans repeat behaviors
that are reinforced by rewards and cease behaviors that have
"punishing" outcomes. Reinforcement can be of two kinds:
the "positive" addition of something pleasing or the "negative"
removal of something unpleasant. Likewise, punishment can be
the "positive" imposition of a penalty or the "negative" removal
of something pleasant—both of which are designed to weaken
unfavorable behavior.

COGNITIVE MAPS

We often gain knowledge without realizing it and only notice what we have learned when a situation prompts us to remember it. In the 1940s, Edward C. Tolman explored this phenomenon, which psychologists call "latent learning." Tolman discovered that rats learn to negotiate complex environments, including mazes, even when there is no incentive for them to do so (a food reward, for example). He argued that rats unconsciously form mental images, or "cognitive maps," of their surroundings, which they then use for navigation. He suggested that the same is true of humans and that many of our learning processes are similarly unconscious.

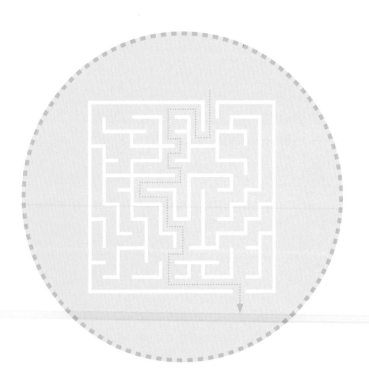

Behaviorism
Behavioral psychologists focus their research on how people behave, rather than how they think, when they respond to particular stimuli.

BRIDGING THE GAP

Behavioral psychologists (see pp.32–35) use a two-stage "in–out" model to explore how external stimuli (input) affect human behavior (output). They pay little attention to any mental activity that might occur inside the brain. By contrast, cognitive behaviorists propose that there is an intermediate stage, in which brain-based cognitive processes (see pp.86–105) enable us to experience the world, acquire knowledge, and reinterpret our perceptions. Their model has three stages: "in–internal processing–out."

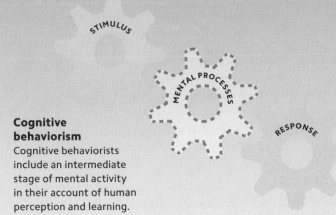

Cognitive behaviorism
Cognitive behaviorists include an intermediate stage of mental activity in their account of human perception and learning.

ESTEEM

LOVE AND BELONGING

SAFETY

PHYSIOLOGICAL

THE HIERARCHY OF NEEDS

Abraham Maslow suggested that we are motivated by five basic needs, which in turn need to be satisfied in a particular order. Physiological needs (such as food, sleep, and water) are necessary for survival, so we must fulfill them first. Second, we need safety, in the form of shelter and protection from harm. Third, we need loving relationships and a sense of community. Fourth, we need esteem, or a sense of being respected by other people. Finally, we need to make full use of our talents and abilities in order to achieve our true potential. Maslow called this process "self-actualization" and believed that not all of us are able to fulfill this final need.

Unconditional support
Rogers believed that
therapists should offer their
client complete acceptance,
no matter what the client
says or does.

COMPLETE SUPPORT AND ACCEPTANCE

Maslow's idea that self-actualization is one of our five basic needs (see opposite) was inspired by the work of his contemporary Carl Rogers, who pioneered the humanistic approach to psychology (see p.131). Rogers believed that people are fundamentally good and that we should accept ourselves unconditionally. As a therapist, he offered his clients what he called "unconditional positive regard"— that is, complete support and acceptance. By doing so, he hoped to uproot a major cause of anxiety within individuals—namely, our belief that we are only acceptable if we live up to certain expectations.

**Unconditional
self-acceptance**
Many people's anxiety
is lifted when they
recognize that they are
acceptable for who
they truly are.

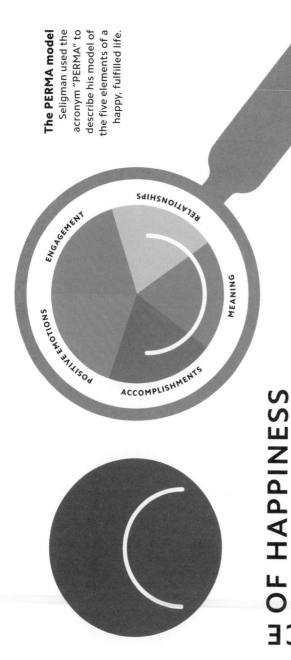

RELATIONSHIPS

ENGAGEMENT

MEANING

POSITIVE EMOTIONS

ACCOMPLISHMENTS

THE SCIENCE OF HAPPINESS

Abraham Maslow (see p.38) coined the term "positive psychology" in 1954, when he proposed that by merely examining mental disorders, psychologists gain no insight into human potential. Instead, he argued that they should study mentally healthy people in order to identify what best promotes good, happy, and healthy living. Martin Seligman later built on Maslow's ideas, proposing that there are three types of happy life: the "pleasant life," involving sensual pleasure and socializing; the "meaningful life," doing things for others; and the "good life," in which we fulfill our own potential for personal growth.

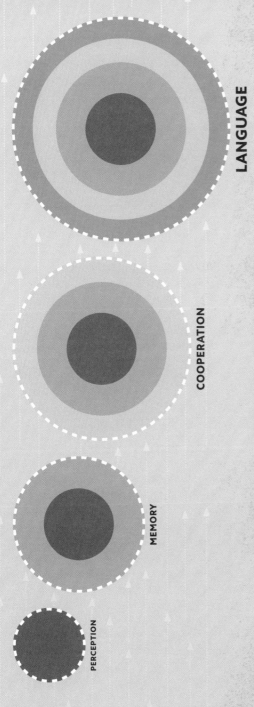

LANGUAGE

COOPERATION

MEMORY

PERCEPTION

THE MIND EVOLVED

Evolutionary psychologists believe that studying humans as part of the general evolution of life forms on Earth provides insights into psychology. Pointing out that if a physical trait helps a life form to survive, it persists due to natural selection, they suggest that mental processes and behavior also evolve in the same way. For example, our ancestors' ability to be aware of environmental stimuli may have provoked basic reactions, but not learning. The capacity for memory and recall would have boosted their chances of survival, as would developing cooperative behavior and, finally, language.

> "The mind is an adaptation designed by natural selection."
> Steven Pinker

This deepest part of our brains prompts us to satisfy our most fundamental needs, such as the need to eat and to reproduce.

LIMBIC SYSTEM

CEREBRAL CORTEX

This outermost, folded part of our brains plays a key role in our "higher" mental processes, such as planning, imagining, and making decisions.

NERVE NETWORK

A system of nerves connects our brains to the rest of our bodies via our spinal columns. This enables our brains to guide and monitor our behavior.

Control systems

Our bodies are controlled by two main systems: a network of nerves and an array of chemical messengers called "hormones."

Our nerves are made up of millions of cells called "neurons." These cells communicate with each other using chemicals called "neurotransmitters," enabling them to pass messages to and from our brains.

NEURON

Biopsychology combines the study of anatomy (bodily structure), physiology (bodily functions), and psychology. Biopsychologists study how our brains and nervous systems influence the ways in which we think, feel, and behave and try to pinpoint how mental functions are linked to particular parts of our brains. In doing so, they focus on nerve cells, or "neurons," which carry information from our senses to our brains and relay instructions from our brains to other parts of our bodies. They also study how other chemicals, called "hormones," prime us to behave in particular ways.

BIOLOGICAL BEHAVIOR

Hormones are chemicals that travel in our blood. They control many of our bodily functions, including our emotional reactions and our ability to digest food.

HORMONE

GROWTH

AND

DEVELO

PMENT

Before the 1930s, most psychologists thought that we learn by adjusting our behavior in order to pursue rewards or avoid punishment (see pp.32–35). However, in 1936, Jean Piaget challenged this idea: he proposed that we pass through four stages of development and that the way we learn is different in each stage (see p.47). A new branch of psychology, known as developmental psychology, emerged from his work. Its researchers focus on the ways in which we change psychologically at different times in our lives and on the extent to which our learning is shaped by genetic, environmental, or social factors.

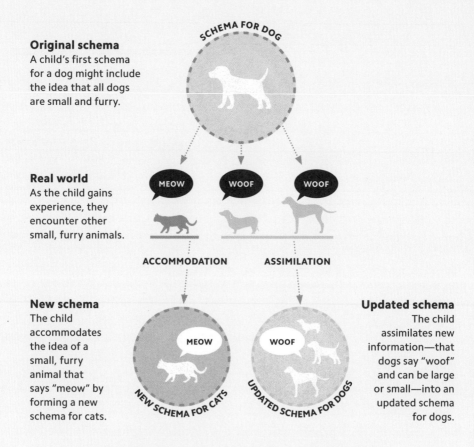

Original schema
A child's first schema for a dog might include the idea that all dogs are small and furry.

SCHEMA FOR DOG

Real world
As the child gains experience, they encounter other small, furry animals.

MEOW

WOOF

WOOF

ACCOMMODATION

ASSIMILATION

New schema
The child accommodates the idea of a small, furry animal that says "meow" by forming a new schema for cats.

MEOW

NEW SCHEMA FOR CATS

WOOF

UPDATED SCHEMA FOR DOGS

Updated schema
The child assimilates new information—that dogs say "woof" and can be large or small—into an updated schema for dogs.

ORGANIZING IDEAS

Jean Piaget described a child's mental development as an increase in the number and complexity of "schemas," the basic building blocks of intelligence that help us understand and interpret the world. Schemas enable us to organize and categorize knowledge by dividing it into units that relate to different aspects of the world, such as actions, objects, or abstract concepts. They remain stored in our minds, and we apply them when needed, which enables us to sort through vast amounts of information quickly.

HOW CHILDREN THINK

Piaget (see opposite) also developed the theory that children move through four different stages of cognitive development as they grow up: the sensorimotor stage, the preoperational stage, the operational stage, and the formal operational stage. He proposed that children's minds are not just a smaller, though fully formed, version of an adult mind, but that their intelligence develops through these four stages. His work showed that there are differences both in the kind of thinking and the amount of thinking that children perform at the different stages of their development.

H_2O

WATER

Sensorimotor (birth–24 months)
Infants experience the world through movement and sensation, such as by grasping things or sucking them.

Preoperational (2–7 years)
As language develops, children learn to use words and pictures to represent concrete (real) objects or simple concepts, such as "water."

Operational (7–11 years)
Children begin to use logic and learn more complex concepts, such as "conservation" (the idea that differently shaped cups can hold the same amount of liquid).

Formal operational (12 years+)
Adolescents gain the ability to think in the abstract—that is, to visualize things that they cannot see in the real world (such as water molecules) and use reasoning to understand them.

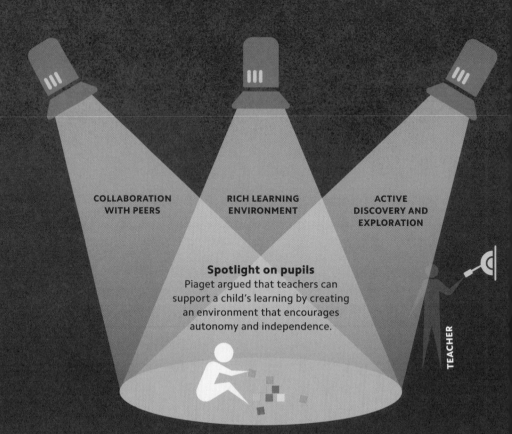

COLLABORATION WITH PEERS

RICH LEARNING ENVIRONMENT

ACTIVE DISCOVERY AND EXPLORATION

Spotlight on pupils
Piaget argued that teachers can support a child's learning by creating an environment that encourages autonomy and independence.

TEACHER

A NATURAL PROCESS

In the early 20th century, Jean Piaget argued that children develop naturally and learn independently by encountering new experiences. He therefore proposed a "child-centered" approach to education. His method requires teachers to consider a child's individual learning style, abilities, requirements, and interests. Teachers then make learning easier by fostering an environment of trust and confidence within which the child can actively explore, participate, and experiment.

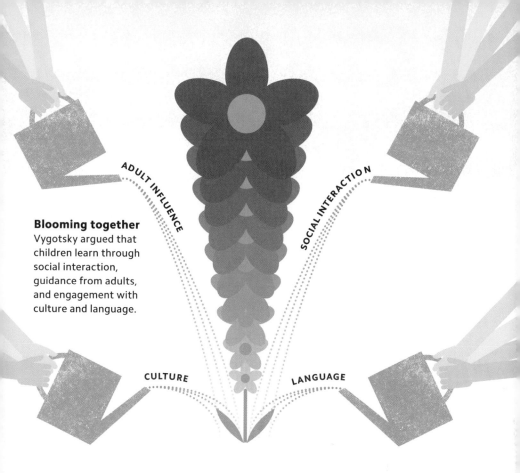

Blooming together
Vygotsky argued that children learn through social interaction, guidance from adults, and engagement with culture and language.

ADULT INFLUENCE

SOCIAL INTERACTION

CULTURE

LANGUAGE

LEARNING TOGETHER

In the 1930s, Lev Vygotsky argued that children learn by interacting with adults and peers and that their cognitive development is heavily influenced by both language and culture. Unlike Jean Piaget (see opposite), Vygotsky believed that each child has a set of potential abilities that can only be unlocked by collaborating with others. He suggested that children learn best in the "Zone of Proximal Development"—that is, when they are working on tasks that they can only master with guidance and support.

THE EIGHT STAGES
OF HUMAN LIFE

Erik Erikson developed one of the most influential theories about human personality. He argued that, as we grow older, we pass through eight stages of development. During each stage, we encounter a conflict, which can have a positive or negative outcome. For example, in the first stage (from birth up to 18 months), we experience a conflict in which we learn whether or not to trust our caregivers. If we learn that they are trustworthy, we develop a belief that our needs will be met, and therefore a sense of hope. If we pass through all eight stages successfully, we gain what Erikson called the "virtues," or characteristics, of healthy adults.

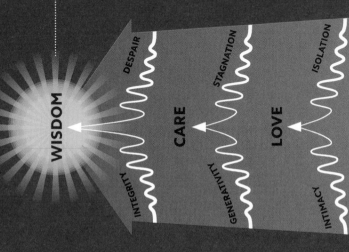

A healthy adult has successfully passed through all eight stages. They feel secure and unregretful.
ATTAINING WISDOM

WISDOM

INTEGRITY

DESPAIR

CARE

GENERATIVITY

STAGNATION

LOVE

INTIMACY

ISOLATION

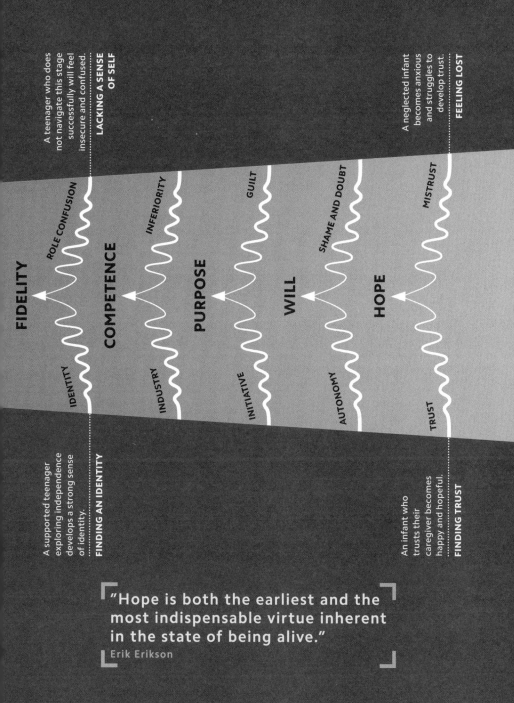

A teenager who does not navigate this stage successfully will feel insecure and confused.

LACKING A SENSE OF SELF

A neglected infant becomes anxious and struggles to develop trust.

FEELING LOST

FIDELITY

ROLE CONFUSION

IDENTITY

COMPETENCE

INFERIORITY

INDUSTRY

PURPOSE

GUILT

INITIATIVE

WILL

SHAME AND DOUBT

AUTONOMY

HOPE

MISTRUST

TRUST

A supported teenager exploring independence develops a strong sense of identity.

FINDING AN IDENTITY

An infant who trusts their caregiver becomes happy and hopeful.

FINDING TRUST

"Hope is both the earliest and the most indispensable virtue inherent in the state of being alive."
Erik Erikson

INSTINCTIVE BEHAVIOR

In the 1930s, zoologist Konrad Lorenz studied "fixed-action patterns," the instinctive behaviors wired into the nervous systems of animals. During experiments, he noticed that baby geese follow the first living thing they see after hatching, even a human. This is known as "imprinting." Lorenz also observed that a specific stimulus can trigger a fixed-action pattern: for instance, when he placed an egg by a mother goose's nest, she always completed the same routine to retrieve it, even if he removed the egg before she had finished. Lorenz concluded that fixed-action patterns are not learned, but are genetically programmed. This raises the question of how many human behaviors, such as babies' attachment to their caregivers, are similarly hardwired.

INNATE TRIGGER

An animal's genes are programmed so that when the animal receives a particular stimulus, it performs a fixed-action pattern from start to finish, regardless of context.

GENETICALLY PROGRAMMED

Animals have complex, species-specific instincts and behaviors that are hardwired into their neural networks.

ADULT HITS TOY

CHILD OBSERVES ADULT

COPYING OTHERS

In the 1960s, Albert Bandura questioned the behaviorist theory that all learning is a result of direct experience and reinforcement (see pp.32–35). Instead, he proposed a "social learning theory," arguing that people learn behaviors by observing and copying others. In a well-known experiment, he showed that children can learn to behave aggressively through imitating adults. He argued that such learning can also take place indirectly, raising fears that children may learn from behavior that they see on TV or online.

CHILD IMITATES ADULT'S BEHAVIOR

"Bobo doll" experiment
In this experiment, children saw an adult act violently toward a toy called "Bobo." Later, they also behaved aggressively with Bobo.

EARLY RELATIONSHIPS

After working with emotionally disturbed children, John Bowlby decided to study the relationships between young children and their mothers, focusing on social, emotional, and cognitive development. He concluded that children are biologically preprogrammed to form attachments with caregivers, who will help them survive. He also proposed that infants are born with the need to attach to a single primary figure, which is often the mother. Bowlby believed that children make this attachment during the first five years of their lives, after which it may never form.

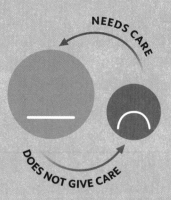

Strong attachment
A child develops a strong attachment to a nurturing caregiver. This gives the child confidence to explore their environment.

No attachment
A child does not form an attachment to a neglectful caregiver. Subsequently, the child grows up feeling lost and insecure.

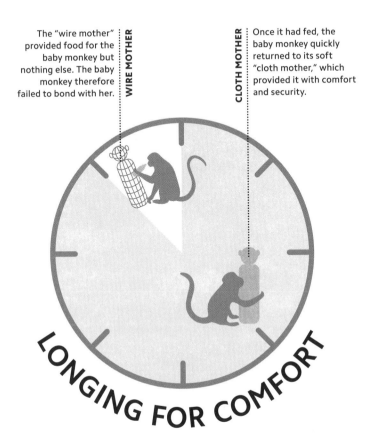

WIRE MOTHER

The "wire mother" provided food for the baby monkey but nothing else. The baby monkey therefore failed to bond with her.

CLOTH MOTHER

Once it had fed, the baby monkey quickly returned to its soft "cloth mother," which provided it with comfort and security.

LONGING FOR COMFORT

In the 1960s, many psychologists theorized that babies form attachments to their mothers simply because they need to be fed. Harry Harlow suspected that comfort and love were just as important to an infant, and tested this theory using monkeys. He separated several baby monkeys from their mothers and gave them two surrogate mothers each: one that provided milk but was made of wire and one that was made of terrycloth. The babies spent most of their time with their "cloth mothers" and only briefly went to their "wire mothers" to feed. This proved that infants have a strong need for comfort from their caregivers.

FEELING SECURE

Mary Ainsworth devised a way of classifying the relationships between children and their primary caregivers. In an experiment known as the Strange Situation, Ainsworth left several mother-and-child pairs in an unfamiliar room, in which the child was free to play. She then observed the child's responses to various potentially stressful situations, including being left alone for a couple of minutes and seeing a stranger enter the room. Based on how each child reacted, Ainsworth defined three kinds of child-caregiver attachment: "secure," "insecure ambivalent," and "insecure avoidant".

"Infants who were ... securely attached to their mothers explored actively."
Mary Ainsworth

Constant mothers
The researchers asked each mother to behave in the same way during the test. Each one let her child explore the room before leaving it alone for a brief period of time.

Secure
The child explored the room, using its mother as a secure base. It was unhappy to be left alone but happy when its mother returned.

Insecure ambivalent
The child did not explore the room and rejected its mother's attempts to encourage and comfort it.

Insecure avoidant
The child showed independence and explored the room. It did not go to its mother for security.

ABUSER

Child with high-activity MAOA gene
A maltreated child with high levels of MAOA
activity is less likely to develop antisocial
behavior as an adult.

OTHER PERSON

RESPONSES TO ABUSE

Some people who are physically or sexually abused as children go
on to display disruptive or violent behavior as adults. In 2002,
Avshalom Caspi presented evidence suggesting that the activity
levels of the "MAOA" gene can affect the way in which maltreated
children react to their experiences; this gene controls production
of monoamine oxidase A, an enzyme that breaks down some
neurotransmitters (see p.42). Caspi's work suggests that genetics
may explain why not all victims of abuse go on to abuse others.

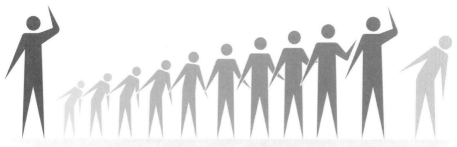

ABUSER

Child with low-activity MAOA gene
A maltreated child with low levels of MAOA
activity is more likely to develop antisocial
behavior as an adult.

OTHER PERSON

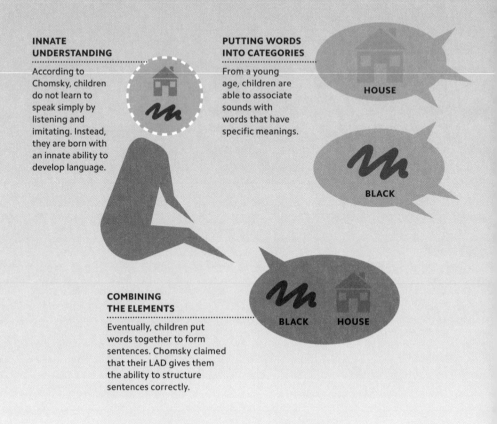

INNATE UNDERSTANDING

According to Chomsky, children do not learn to speak simply by listening and imitating. Instead, they are born with an innate ability to develop language.

PUTTING WORDS INTO CATEGORIES

From a young age, children are able to associate sounds with words that have specific meanings.

HOUSE

BLACK

COMBINING THE ELEMENTS

Eventually, children put words together to form sentences. Chomsky claimed that their LAD gives them the ability to structure sentences correctly.

BLACK   HOUSE

BORN TO SPEAK

Language is incredibly complex, and yet most children master its rules by the age of 8. In the 1960s, linguist Noam Chomsky suggested that the human brain has a specialized "Language Acquisition Device" (LAD): a mental faculty that enables infants to understand the grammar and syntax of their native language without formal training. This faculty contains what Chomsky called a "universal grammar," which all languages have in common. He argued that when a child hears people speak, its LAD becomes active, enabling it to respond appropriately.

RIGHT OR WRONG?

In 1958, Lawrence Kohlberg proposed that humans pass through three stages of moral development, each of which has two phases. He argued that we move through these stages in a particular order and that moral development is linked to cognitive development. In the first stage, we have what Kohlberg called "preconventional" morals, which are shaped by our awareness of obedience and punishment and of individualism and exchange. In the second stage, we embrace "conventional" morals, driven by our need for good personal relationships and our awareness of the need for social order. In the third, "postconventional" stage, we consider more general moral issues, such as the existence of human rights.

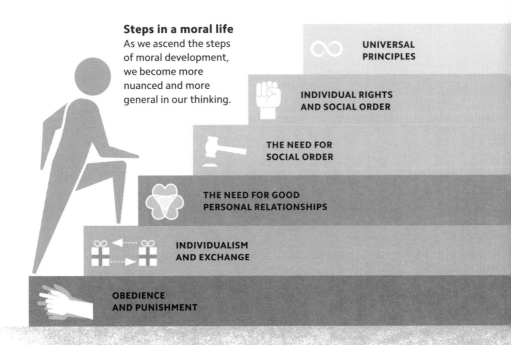

Steps in a moral life
As we ascend the steps of moral development, we become more nuanced and more general in our thinking.

UNIVERSAL PRINCIPLES

INDIVIDUAL RIGHTS AND SOCIAL ORDER

THE NEED FOR SOCIAL ORDER

THE NEED FOR GOOD PERSONAL RELATIONSHIPS

INDIVIDUALISM AND EXCHANGE

OBEDIENCE AND PUNISHMENT

THE DOLL TESTS

Kenneth and Mamie Clark were a married couple who studied children's attitudes toward race. During the 1940s, they conducted experiments in the US, in which they asked African American children to choose between two dolls that were identical, aside from hair and skin color. Results showed a clear preference for the white doll over the brown doll, which suggested that these children had internalized racist attitudes due to segregation and social influences. The Clarks' work contributed to the 1954 Supreme Court's ruling that allowing racial segregation in public education was unconstitutional.

DOLL WITH WHITE SKIN

Most of the children associated the white doll with being "nice" and "good," expressing a clear preference for it.

DOLL WITH BROWN SKIN

59 percent of the children said that the brown doll "looks bad," revealing internalized racism.

AFRICAN AMERICAN CHILD

"To separate them from others of similar age and qualifications solely because of their race generates a feeling of inferiority."

Chief Justice
Earl Warren

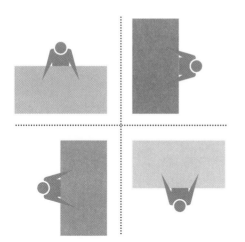

Conflict
A competitive classroom setting, combined with racial hostilities, encouraged students to discriminate against each other.

REDUCING PREJUDICE

In 1971, Elliot Aronson was asked to advise desegregated schools on how to counter the fighting, discrimination, and hate crimes that had become endemic. Aronson developed the "Jigsaw Classroom," a teaching technique designed to reduce racial prejudice and facilitate learning. Teachers divided the classroom into diversified groups and broke up assignments into pieces that the group had to assemble like a jigsaw puzzle. This made students rely on each other to complete their task and reduced instances of prejudice and stereotyping.

Cooperation
Aronson designed the Jigsaw Classroom to create a cooperative environment. This enabled students to meet their team goals by working together as a group.

EXPLORING ETHNICITY

In the 1980s, Jean Phinney investigated the process by which young people from minority ethnic groups come to understand their racial and cultural identities. She proposed that individuals undergo three stages of development: the "unexamined ethnic identity" stage, the "ethnic identity search/moratorium" stage (in which they examine their cultural heritage), and the "ethnic identity achievement" stage (in which they understand and accept their identities). More recently, researchers have formed the "Ethnic and Racial Identity in the 21st Century Study Group," which reviews and builds on the work of Phinney and others.

Unexamined identity
A child may not examine their ethnicity and instead may unconsciously accept the values of the society in which they live.

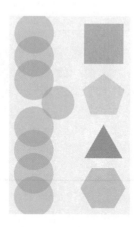

Identity search
As an adolescent, the same person may encounter a number of ethnic identities and search for their own sense of identity.

Identity achievement
Most adults understand and accept their ethnic identity, as well as the differences between their ethnic group and society at large.

Fostering femininity
Parents often bring up girls to dress in "feminine" colors, such as pink; give them "feminine" toys, such as dolls; and encourage them to look "pretty."

Challenging norms
Parents and teachers can help children challenge gender norms by talking to them about stereotypes and by avoiding treating them in gendered ways.

Fostering masculinity
Parents often dress boys in "masculine" colors, such as blue; give them "masculine" toys, such as trucks; and encourage them to be "strong" and "brave."

BOY OR GIRL?

Traditionally, psychologists believed that hardwired, biological differences between the brains of men and women determine differences in their feelings and behavior. However, research has shown that, although most people are born with either a male or a female body, the cultural environment in which they grow up has a greater impact on whether they develop stereotypically "masculine" or "feminine" feelings or behaviors. For this reason, most psychologists now distinguish between a person's physical sex (usually either male or female) and their gender (whether they consider themselves to be a man, a woman, both, or neither).

GENDER

STEREOTYPES

In the early
1970s, Eleanor Maccoby
observed that scientific studies
around sex and gender tended to
emphasize differences between females
and males instead of similarities. Seeking to
challenge gender stereotypes, Maccoby explored
the biological, cognitive, and social factors that
contribute to sex differences. She found that
biological influences are not as important as
psychologists believed: parental, social,
and cultural influences have just as
much impact.

"... most of what we think about as
differences, essential differences
between the sexes, are myths."
Eleanor Maccoby

In the 1970s, Lorna Wing suggested that autism exists on a spectrum (see p.110). Later, researchers questioned why autism seems to occur more frequently in males. In 2002, Simon Baron-Cohen theorized that exposure to testosterone in the womb contributes to cognitive sex differences and that, on average, the "female" brain is programmed to empathize and the "male" brain to systemize. His "extreme male brain" theory proposed that people with autism have more "systemizing" brains (although he stressed that this does not mean that they are "hyper-male" or incapable of empathy).

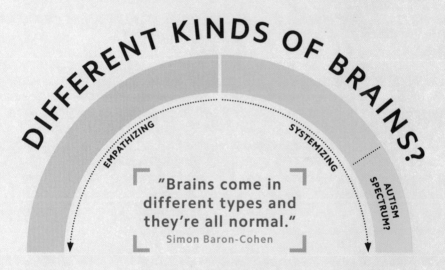

DIFFERENT KINDS OF BRAINS?

EMPATHIZING

SYSTEMIZING

AUTISM SPECTRUM?

"Brains come in different types and they're all normal."
Simon Baron-Cohen

More recent studies have cast some doubt on Baron-Cohen's theory, and other researchers have challenged it. And so, scientists are still investigating the relationship between sex, gender, childhood development, and autism: in particular, why males are often diagnosed earlier in life (see p.110) and how autism intersects with gender diversity.

SELF
AND
SOCI

E T Y

In the early 20th century, experimental psychologists mainly studied the thoughts and behavior of individuals. However, it became increasingly clear that how we think and behave is greatly influenced by how we interact with other people, and the field of social psychology was developed to study this influence. Social psychologists examine the ways in which individuals are affected by society, looking in particular at the nature of prejudice, persuasion, conformity, and obedience and at the ways in which people relate both in groups and one-on-one. Their work has influenced many aspects of society, from creating safer communities to team-building in sports.

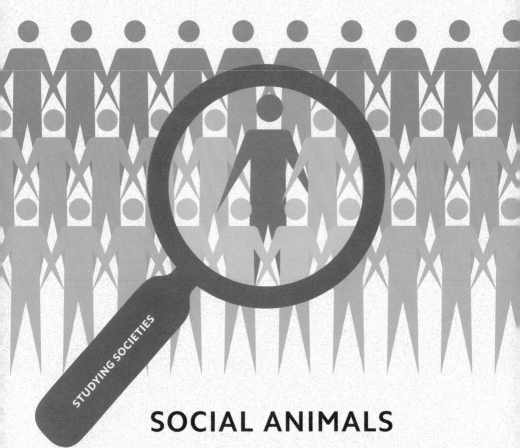

SOCIAL ANIMALS

In the early 20th century, John Dewey argued that human beings are essentially social in nature and that psychologists should therefore study societies rather than individuals. Following the naturalist Charles Darwin, Dewey proposed that our minds, like our bodies, are a product of evolution and that we have evolved to cooperate with each other. Overturning centuries of thinking, Dewey argued further that our minds do not passively observe the world, but actively engage with it, and adapt to our social and cultural environments.

THE LIFE SPACE

In the 1940s, Kurt Lewin argued that psychologists should study how individuals interact with the world as they perceive it to be. Known as field theory, his work analyzes people in terms of their entire physical, social, and psychological environment, which he called their "life space." Lewin compared this space to a field in which "psychical forces," including assumptions about the world, shape the way each of us acts. For Lewin, human behavior is the result of an active interplay between a person and their environment, and so can only be understood in particular, individual contexts.

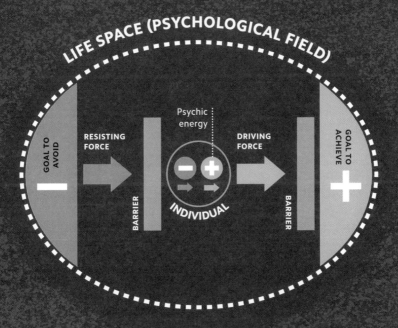

Psychic tension
According to Lewin, our life spaces contain tensions between what we want to achieve and what we want to avoid, and we must constantly try to overcome barriers to success.

Overlapping categories
Researchers such as Sari van Anders
suggest that each person's sexuality has
many interrelated aspects, including (but
not limited to) preferences about gender,
sex, and number of partners.

RESEARCHING SEXUALITY

In 1948, Alfred Kinsey produced one of the first psychological
studies of sexual orientation. While progressive at the time, it limited
sexuality to seven categories, including homosexual, heterosexual,
and bisexual. Today, the concept of sexual orientation has widened
to incorporate multiple expressions of sexuality, with a focus on
determining factors such as how a person self-identifies, as well as
their sexual attractions, behavior, fantasies, and general lifestyle.
Some researchers no longer consider sexuality to be a rigid concept
and instead suggest that it has many different dimensions, which
they are working to describe and explain.

THE KINSEY SCALE

| 0 | 1 | 2 | 3 | 4 | 5 | 6 |

HETEROSEXUAL ◄••••••••••••••••••••••••••••••► HOMOSEXUAL

Sexual continuum
Kinsey designed a seven-point scale that
placed sexuality on a continuum. He
proposed that sexual orientation was
fluid and changeable over time.

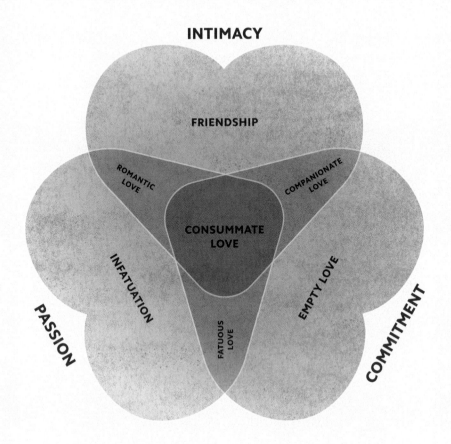

INTIMACY

FRIENDSHIP

ROMANTIC LOVE

COMPANIONATE LOVE

CONSUMMATE LOVE

INFATUATION

FATUOUS LOVE

EMPTY LOVE

PASSION

COMMITMENT

SEVEN KINDS OF LOVE

Robert Sternberg's triangular theory of love describes how interpersonal relationships consist of three key elements: intimacy, passion, and commitment. He states that each element is distinct, but all three are interrelated and can be experienced to varying degrees in a relationship. Sternberg argues that they give rise to seven types of love when combined in different ways and that these can shift over time. He also describes "consummate love" as the ideal form of love, because it includes all three elements.

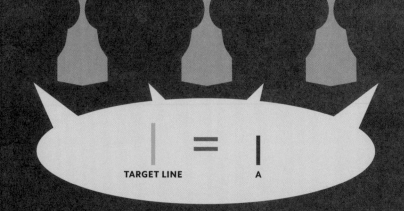

MAJORITY RULES

In 1951, Solomon Asch conducted a series of experiments that demonstrated that people can be influenced by the behavior of others. He placed individual volunteers in groups of actors, who knew the real aim of the experiment but pretended to be fellow volunteers. Each group was then presented with a card on which lines of various lengths had been drawn. When they were asked which of the lines was the same length as a "target line," the actors identified the incorrect line. Although the true volunteers knew that their fellow "volunteers" were mistaken, the majority of them chose to agree with the wrong answer.

AUTHORITY FIGURES

In the 1960s, Stanley Milgram performed an experiment in which a group of researchers persuaded numerous individual volunteers to question a test subject and to punish him with increasingly severe electric shocks if he failed to respond correctly. Although they were reluctant to do so, more than half of the volunteers delivered the electric shocks. In reality, the electric shocks were faked, and the subject receiving them was an actor. However, the experiment showed that, in certain circumstances, people can easily be persuaded to act against their own consciences. Milgram believed that we are all primed from an early age to obey authority figures.

"Ordinary people ... without any particular hostility on their part, can become agents in a terrible destructive process."
Stanley Milgram

THE PERCEPTION OF POWER

In 1971, Philip Zimbardo set out to understand how we behave when we believe that we have power over others. He recruited volunteers to take part in an experiment that simulated a prison setting and assigned each one a role as either a prison guard or a prisoner. Despite knowing that they were part of an experiment, the participants took their roles seriously, and their behavior underwent intense changes: for example, the guards showed uncharacteristic amounts of aggression. The experiment was terminated early due to concerns about the well-being of the prisoners, who quickly showed signs of emotional distress.

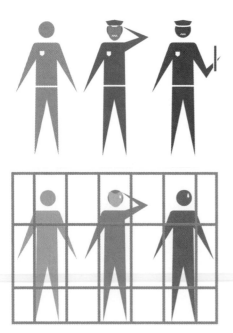

Guards
All the guards took their roles very seriously. They threatened the prisoners physically and insisted that they perform menial tasks, such as scrubbing the toilets with their hands.

Prisoners
Some of the prisoners fixated on abiding by the prison rules, even to the point of turning against their fellow prisoners. Others rebelled by barricading themselves inside their cells.

CONTEXT MATTERS

Writing in 1972, Elliot Aronson suggested that we often behave in ways that do not reflect our true personalities. Instead, he argued, we are influenced by powerful social forces that play a much larger role in our lives than we would like to admit. According to Aronson, in order to understand someone who is behaving unusually, psychologists need to consider their behavior within its wider social context rather than simply examining their personality to see where they "went wrong." He expressed this observation in what he called "Aronson's First Law": "People who do crazy things are not necessarily crazy."

"Crazy"
When a person behaves in an unusual way, others might assume that there is something wrong with their personality.

Not-so-crazy
A person's unusual behavior may not appear so "crazy," however, when seen within the social context that gives rise to it.

COMPETING FOR RESOURCES

In the 1950s, Muzafer Sherif devised the "Robber's Cave" experiment to investigate what happens when two groups of boys are brought together to compete for specific goals. Sherif found that conflict between the groups increases when there can only be one winning side. However, when a goal is best achieved through collaboration, conflict decreases and the groups join forces to work together.

Conflict
When a goal is in limited supply, so only one side can win, the two groups come into conflict.

Cooperation
When achieving a common goal requires collaboration, the two groups put conflict aside.

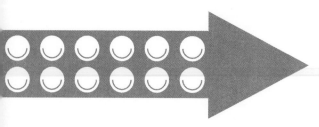

Many bystanders

Individuals in a group are less likely to help in an emergency. Each feels a decreased sense of responsibility.

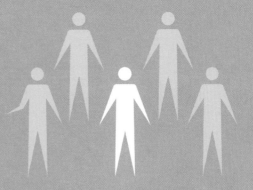

EMERGENCY

AVOIDING RESPONSIBILITY

First proposed in 1964, the "bystander effect" is a theory that suggests that an individual who is part of a group of bystanders is less likely than a lone individual to help a stranger in an emergency. In 1968, John Darley and Bibb Latané argued that this occurs because people are afraid of being embarrassed if they misread a situation and because they assume that other people are better qualified to help than they are. Darley and Latané called this phenomenon "diffusion of responsibility."

Single bystander

Lone individuals are more likely to help in an emergency. They feel an increased sense of personal responsibility.

EMERGENCY

PREFERRING THE FAMILIAR

During the second half of the 20th century, Robert Zajonc found that after he had exposed people repeatedly to a specific object, they preferred that object over others. Based on his findings, Zajonc concluded that when an object is familiar to us, we tend to like it more. He named this tendency "the mere-exposure effect." He repeated his studies using different stimuli—such as paintings, words, symbols, and music—and all showed similar results, with individuals showing a preference for familiar stimuli.

INITIAL EXPOSURE

Zajonc showed participants a series of objects, one of which appeared multiple times.

PREFERENCE

When Zajonc asked the participants which of the objects they preferred, they chose the one that they had seen the most often.

"Bad things happen to bad people"
According to just-world theory, if a person is suffering, they must have done something to deserve it.

"Good things happen to good people"
Likewise, according to the same theory, if a person enjoys a happy life, they must be a good person.

THEIR JUST DESERTS?

In the mid-20th century, Melvin Lerner investigated the "just-world" hypothesis: our human need to believe that the world is fair and that any injustices in it are explicable. Lerner argued that we try to protect ourselves from the threat of an unjust world by adopting the belief that "people get what they deserve." By believing that good things happen to good people and that bad things happen only to bad people, we can convince ourselves that justice is served—even if, in reality, it is not. Furthermore, if we believe that someone's misfortune is a result of their own behavior, we can reassure ourselves that the same misfortune will not befall us, as long as we avoid that behavior.

MAKING ASSUMPTIONS

In the early 1950s, Gordon Allport explored the psychological process behind prejudice and developed a theory that prejudice occurs when we categorize people into separate social groups. Although categorizing in this way allows our brains to simplify incoming information, it can also lead to us creating stereotypes. For example, we may mistakenly assume that all members of a particular social group display certain negative characteristics. This can then influence how we treat members of that group. Allport argued that it is vital to challenge these sorts of assumptions, and his work encouraged some governments to introduce anti-discriminatory policies and laws.

Negative stereotype
Allport described prejudice as a hostile attitude held toward an individual solely because they belong to a group that we perceive negatively.

> "Prejudgments become prejudices only if they are not reversible when exposed to new knowledge."
> Gordon Allport

MEASURING OPINIONS

Devised by Janet T. Spence and Robert L. Helmreich in 1972, the Attitudes Toward Women Scale is a questionnaire that consists of a series of statements about the societal roles and rights of women compared to men. The statements address topics such as vocation, freedom and independence, education, etiquette, sexual behavior, and relationships. Respondents indicate how far they agree or disagree, and researchers score each answer on a scale ranging from "strongly conservative" (traditional) to "egalitarian" (liberal or pro-feminist). Research with the scale has shown that attitudes have become less conservative since it was devised, with women typically holding more egalitarian views than men. Researchers have since developed similar scales to measure attitudes toward trans and gender-nonconforming people.

TRADITIONAL

LIBERAL

STRONGLY
CONSERVATIVE

SOMEWHAT
CONSERVATIVE

SOMEWHAT
EGALITARIAN

STRONGLY
EGALITARIAN

Change management

Kurt Lewin's change management model is a three-step process. During the "unfreeze" stage, leaders explain why change is needed; during the "change" stage, everyone begins to use the new methods; during the "refreeze" stage, employees embrace and implement the change.

UNFREEZE

CHANGE

REFREEZE

Theory X and Theory Y

Douglas McGregor proposed that there are two management styles. "Theory X" managers assume that staff dislike work, so they use authoritarian, hands-on methods. "Theory Y" managers assume that staff enjoy work, so they trust them to work effectively on their own.

X MODEL

Y MODEL

STUDYING ORGANIZATIONS

Organizational psychologists study the behavior of organizations as a whole, as well as the behavior of people within them. They identify principles that govern the behavior of workers, as groups and individuals, and use this to solve problems in the workplace. This may include making changes to an organization's culture so that employees can work more effectively or helping managers recruit and retain staff. Observing and modifying the behavior, dynamics, and systems of an organization are important ways to ensure that it functions at its best. Psychologists use many theories to help with this process, three of which are shown here.

Organizational justice
Jerald Greenberg used the term "organizational justice" to describe an employee's perception of how fairly their organization treats its workers. A sense of justice promotes good attitudes and behavior; a sense of injustice creates poor attitudes and behavior.

SENSE OF JUSTICE

SENSE OF INJUSTICE

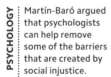

PSYCHOLOGY

Martín-Baró argued that psychologists can help remove some of the barriers that are created by social injustice.

OPPRESSION

According to Martín-Baró, people who have been marginalized in society will often be constrained by social and political factors.

SOCIOPOLITICAL
CONTEXT

EXAMINING OPPRESSION

In the 1980s, Ignacio Martín-Baró declared that psychology is often too Eurocentric in its approach, research, and theories. Liberation psychology, his solution to this problem, aims to amplify the voices and experiences of people who are marginalized by society. His research incorporated the experiences of those oppressed through poverty, corruption, violence, or social injustices. Martín-Baró challenged psychologists to address social injustice and believed that psychology is the key to changing policies that affect people who might be powerless to advocate for themselves.

FREE TO CHOOSE

In 1998, William Glasser developed choice theory. This states that we are free to choose how to behave, even if we are not aware of it, and that we are not able to control other people's behavior—only our own. Glasser argued that we are genetically driven to meet five basic needs (see below), but that we can actively choose how to behave in order to ensure that those needs are met. He considered love to be the most vital of the five needs, believing that we must connect with people in order to fulfill all of our other needs.

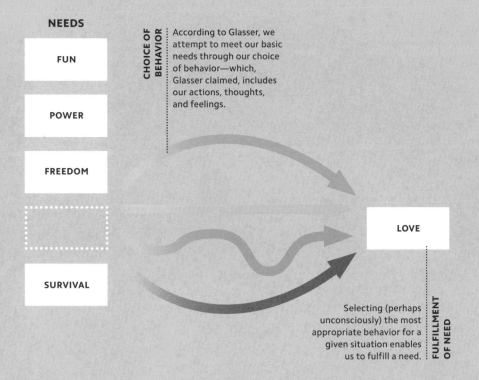

NEEDS

FUN

POWER

FREEDOM

SURVIVAL

CHOICE OF BEHAVIOR

According to Glasser, we attempt to meet our basic needs through our choice of behavior—which, Glasser claimed, includes our actions, thoughts, and feelings.

LOVE

FULFILLMENT OF NEED

Selecting (perhaps unconsciously) the most appropriate behavior for a given situation enables us to fulfill a need.

THOUG
AND
PROCE

H T S

S S E S

In the second half of the 20th century, psychologists began to abandon behaviorism (see pp.32–35) in favor of cognitive psychology: a field of study based on the idea that researchers can study cognition (what goes on in our minds) directly, as opposed to via behavior. It also assumes that our minds are like information processors that run on the hardware (or "wetware") of our brains. Analyzing the mind in this way has led to new insights into many mental processes—including memory, perception, attention, decision-making, and problem-solving—and has even shed light on what it means to be conscious.

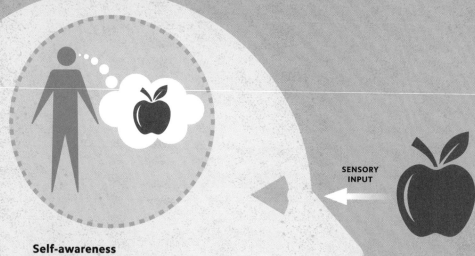

SENSORY INPUT

Self-awareness
A major aspect of consciousness, self-awareness is effectively the state of being aware that we are aware of something.

THE CONSCIOUS MIND

The word "consciousness" has several meanings, ranging from simply being awake to having a sense of "self." Being conscious includes being aware of our thoughts and feelings, as well as the external world of physical objects. However, because consciousness is largely a subjective (personal) experience, it is difficult to define in objective (factual) terms. For this reason, scientists focus on trying to understand what causes consciousness instead of trying to define it.

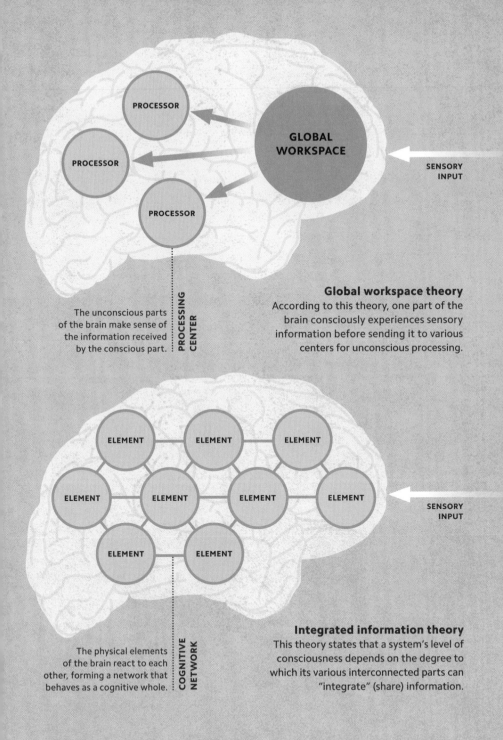

Global workspace theory
According to this theory, one part of the brain consciously experiences sensory information before sending it to various centers for unconscious processing.

The unconscious parts of the brain make sense of the information received by the conscious part.

PROCESSING CENTER

Integrated information theory
This theory states that a system's level of consciousness depends on the degree to which its various interconnected parts can "integrate" (share) information.

The physical elements of the brain react to each other, forming a network that behaves as a cognitive whole.

COGNITIVE NETWORK

PROCESSING
SENSATIONS

Our brains receive information about the world via our sensory organs and nervous systems. We experience this information as sensations, such as sights, sounds, and smells. However, before it can be of use to us, all of this sensory information has to be identified, organized, and interpreted, all of which is done unconsciously by our brains. This process of gathering and structuring sensory information is what psychologists call "perception."

Most psychologists agree that through experience we build up a store of knowledge, including models of the world as we understand it and how we expect it to be.

KNOWLEDGE, MODELS, AND EXPECTATIONS

OBJECT

Organizing information
Perception is the process by which we make sense of the world. Our brains use prior experience to help them identify and organize the information gathered by our senses.

OBJECT

In bottom-up processing, raw, uninterpreted information is sent from our sensory organs to our brains, where it is processed and then interpreted.

DATA-DRIVEN

Bottom-up processing

This occurs when we experience something directly without reference to any prior knowledge, models, or expectations. It is a process of sensation rather than interpretation.

OBJECT

In top-down processing, our brains interpret sensations by applying "schemas," or models of prior experience, to sensory information. This enables us to recognize the world around us.

SCHEMA-DRIVEN

Top-down processing

This type of processing occurs when our brains apply prior knowledge to incoming sensory information. Doing so enables them to organize and interpret our sensations.

Prototype matching

Our brains compare an object with a composite image, or "prototype," which they have compiled based on experiences of similar objects.

Template matching

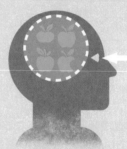

Our brains identify an object by comparing it to various "templates": memories of different examples of similar objects.

Feature analysis

Our brains detect the detailed individual features of an object and compare them to memories of objects with similar features.

Component recognition

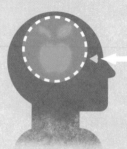

Our brains compare the shapes of component parts of an object, such as the leaves or stalk of an apple, to similar shapes that are stored in our memory.

IDENTIFYING OBJECTS

When we see an object, our brains have to identify what it is. They do so by comparing the object with images of other objects that we have seen before, which are stored in our memories. This process is known as "pattern recognition." Psychologists currently have four different theories to explain how it works (see above).

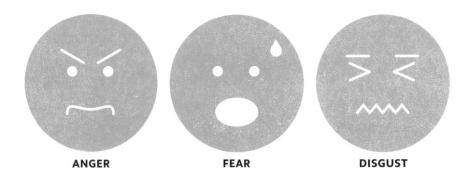

ANGER   **FEAR**   **DISGUST**

BASIC FEELINGS

In the 1970s, Paul Ekman noticed that certain experiences cause us to react involuntarily—such as to jump in fright, to blush, or to cry. These are physical reactions, but they are caused by emotional responses that are also involuntary. Ekman argued that we have six such automatic, or "primary," emotions: anger, fear, disgust, happiness, sadness, and surprise. According to Ekman, each of these feelings produces a distinctive expression on our faces. He theorized that these expressions, which we all display, are not learned responses, but are instinctive, and have evolved over millions of years.

HAPPINESS   **SADNESS**   **SURPRISE**

MAGIC NUMBER SEVEN

In the late 1950s, psychologists shifted toward an approach that viewed cognition as a kind of information processing system (see opposite). One of the pioneers of the new "cognitive psychology" was George Armitage Miller, who argued that short-term memory has a finite capacity of about seven items. He referred to this as "The Magical Number Seven, Plus or Minus Two"—a limitation that creates a potential bottleneck, controlling what can be stored and eventually transferred to long-term memory. Because of this control mechanism, later psychologists widely referred to short-term memory as "working memory."

Capacity of about seven items

Working memory acts as an "executive control," filtering out all but seven items, which can then be moved to long-term memory.

Capacity of about seven chunks

In order to memorize a greater amount of information, our brains organize these items into seven categories of similar things, or "chunks."

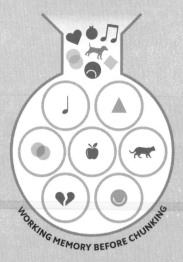

WORKING MEMORY BEFORE CHUNKING

WORKING MEMORY AFTER CHUNKING

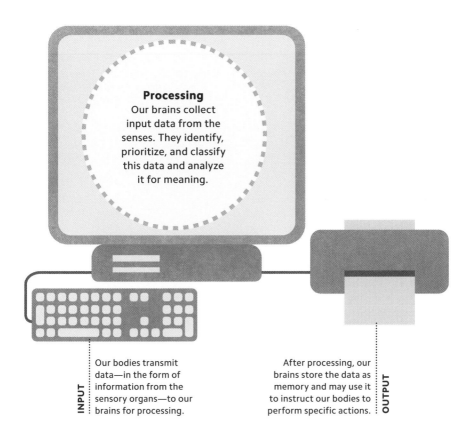

Processing
Our brains collect input data from the senses. They identify, prioritize, and classify this data and analyze it for meaning.

INPUT
Our bodies transmit data—in the form of information from the sensory organs—to our brains for processing.

OUTPUT
After processing, our brains store the data as memory and may use it to instruct our bodies to perform specific actions.

A BIOLOGICAL COMPUTER

In the second half of the 20th century, advances in information technology led researchers to describe the computer as a kind of electronic brain. Similarly, some psychologists proposed that the human brain is like a "biological computer," or information processor. This analogy is a way of describing how our brains process information about the external world and suggests that the distinction between brain and mind is comparable to that between hardware and software. It likens cognitive processes—such as decision-making, storing and recalling memories, and perception—to computer systems.

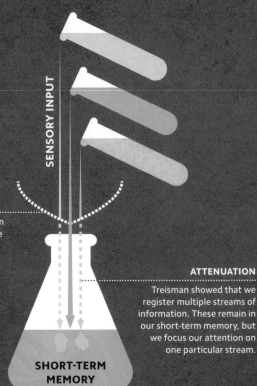

Too much information
Our minds have a limited capacity for processing sensory input. When they are overloaded, they focus our attention on what is most relevant.

SENSORY INPUT

FILTERING
Broadbent proposed that in order to cope with multiple streams of sensory input, we select one as the focus of our attention and filter out the others.

ATTENUATION
Treisman showed that we register multiple streams of information. These remain in our short-term memory, but we focus our attention on one particular stream.

SHORT-TERM MEMORY

FOCUSING ATTENTION

In the 1950s, Donald Broadbent observed that the human mind has a limited ability to deal with all the information it receives from our senses. He argued that our minds have a kind of filter, which focuses our attention on one source of information while filtering out any others. An example of this selective attention is our ability to focus on a single conversation at a noisy party, known as the "cocktail party effect." Anne Treisman built on this idea, proposing that our brains do not fully filter out information that is outside the focus of our attention, but instead "attenuate" it (reduce its significance).

STRIVING FOR CONSISTENCY

Leon Festinger noticed that our beliefs can be so deeply entrenched that they are unshakable, even in the face of solid, contradictory evidence. Furthermore, when there is conflict between the facts and a firmly held belief, it creates an unsettling feeling. Festinger named this state "cognitive dissonance" and claimed it can be eased by rejecting either the belief or the facts. Alternatively, he argued, a person can try to live with dissonance but reduce their exposure to situations that reveal it.

A dissonant state
"Cognitive dissonance" is the state of being torn between a firmly held belief and factual evidence that disproves it.

JUSTIFY EXISTING BELIEF

CHANGE EXISTING BELIEF

REDUCE IMPORTANCE OF PROBLEM

Conflict resolved
When a belief is contradicted by facts, a person can either justify their belief, accept that it is wrong, or minimize the importance of the problem.

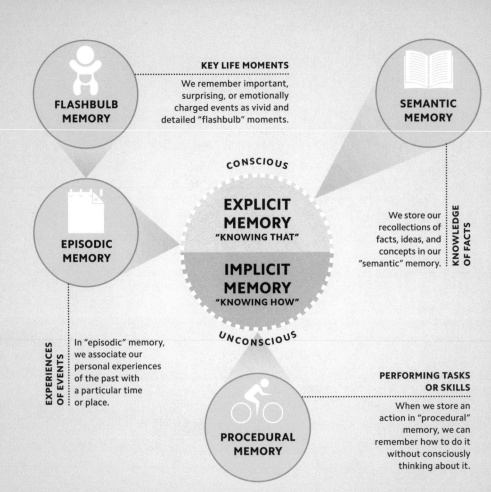

KEY LIFE MOMENTS

We remember important, surprising, or emotionally charged events as vivid and detailed "flashbulb" moments.

FLASHBULB MEMORY

SEMANTIC MEMORY

CONSCIOUS

EXPLICIT MEMORY
"KNOWING THAT"

IMPLICIT MEMORY
"KNOWING HOW"

UNCONSCIOUS

EPISODIC MEMORY

We store our recollections of facts, ideas, and concepts in our "semantic" memory.

KNOWLEDGE OF FACTS

EXPERIENCES OF EVENTS

In "episodic" memory, we associate our personal experiences of the past with a particular time or place.

PERFORMING TASKS OR SKILLS

When we store an action in "procedural" memory, we can remember how to do it without consciously thinking about it.

PROCEDURAL MEMORY

STORAGE STRUCTURE

While our short-term memory has only a limited capacity (see p.94), our long-term memory can store large quantities of information indefinitely. Our minds organize our long-term memories into different categories: in explicit memory, we consciously store and recollect information, while in implicit memory, we do so unconsciously. Explicit memory is further divided into things that we have experienced (episodic memory) and ideas and facts that we have learned (semantic memory).

REWRITING THE PAST

Our memories can be far from reliable. In the 1970s, Elizabeth Loftus conducted research showing that, as well as forgetting details of events in our past, we sometimes recall things differently from the way they actually happened or even "remember" things that did not happen at all. She claimed that we are susceptible to suggestion, and our recollections can be influenced by information—or misinformation—that we gather after an event. For example, her studies showed that asking leading questions in court can affect witness statements. Her work also raised questions about the reliability of memories recovered after traumatic events.

> "Memory works ... like a Wikipedia page: you can go in there and change it, but so can other people."
>
> Elizabeth Loftus

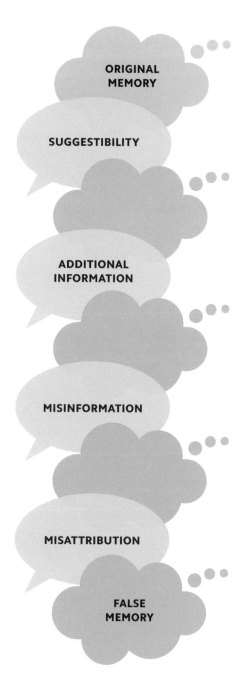

ORIGINAL MEMORY

SUGGESTIBILITY

ADDITIONAL INFORMATION

MISINFORMATION

MISATTRIBUTION

FALSE MEMORY

MEMORY MALFUNCTION

In the 1990s, building on the work of Elizabeth Loftus (see p.99), Daniel Schacter set out to explain how we recall information and how we sometimes introduce inaccuracies into what we remember. He likened the failings of memory to the Seven Deadly Sins and identified seven "sins" of memory. The first three, which he called "sins of omission," occur when an individual cannot recall information. The others, which he termed "sins of commission," occur when an individual recalls corrupted or incorrect information. Although Schacter referred to these events as "sins," he emphasized that they are features of memory rather than faults and can serve a purpose in enabling us to interpret the present and imagine the future.

> "Memory is not a simple replay."
> Daniel Schacter

ORIGINAL MEMORY

Correct memory
When we store a memory correctly, we can completely and accurately recall the original fact or event.

Misattribution
We may recall a memory correctly but attribute that memory to the wrong source.

SINS OF OMISSION (FORGETTING)

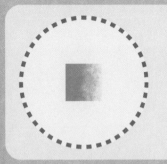 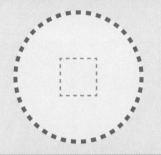 

Transience
Specific memories
can deteriorate over
time. We tend to
remember more
about recent events.

Absent-mindedness
Slips of memory
occur when we do
not pay enough
attention when the
memory is first stored.

Blocking
When we cannot
retrieve a memory,
it may be because
another memory is
obstructing the process.

SINS OF COMMISSION (DISTORTION OR INTRUSION)

Suggestibility
After an event,
suggestions from
other people can
influence and distort
our memories of it.

Bias
Our own mood,
feelings, knowledge,
and opinions can
skew our memories
of past events.

Persistence
Unwanted memories—
of traumatic events, for
example—may persist
in a disturbing and
intrusive way.

FAST AND SLOW DECISIONS

In the 1990s, Daniel Kahneman and Amos Tversky developed a new theory to explain how we make decisions. They proposed that we have two distinct decision-making processes: "fast" (System 1) and "slow" (System 2). Often, they claimed, we have no time to make a fully considered judgment by using the logical System 2, so our brains react to situations instinctively using System 1. This process relies on "heuristics" or "rules of thumb": patterns of information that we can recognize instantly without the need for conscious thought.

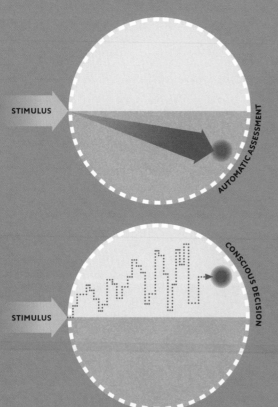

STIMULUS

AUTOMATIC ASSESSMENT

Fast: System 1
In System 1 thinking, the brain reacts to a situation automatically. It involves no conscious thought processes, so the response is immediate.

STIMULUS

CONSCIOUS DECISION

Slow: System 2
In System 2 thinking, the reaction time is much slower, because the brain consciously considers the situation and all its implications before responding.

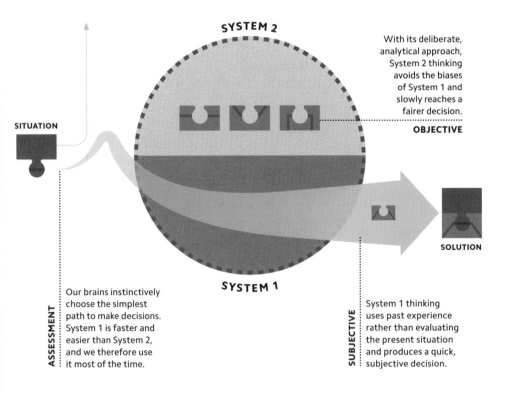

SYSTEM 2

With its deliberate, analytical approach, System 2 thinking avoids the biases of System 1 and slowly reaches a fairer decision.

OBJECTIVE

SITUATION

ASSESSMENT

Our brains instinctively choose the simplest path to make decisions. System 1 is faster and easier than System 2, and we therefore use it most of the time.

SYSTEM 1

SUBJECTIVE

System 1 thinking uses past experience rather than evaluating the present situation and produces a quick, subjective decision.

SOLUTION

JUMPING TO CONCLUSIONS

Heuristics (see opposite), or "rules of thumb," are a feature of System 1 thinking. They are useful for making quick decisions but can lead to unjustified conclusions. In part, this is because, by their nature, heuristics are often biased—that is, they place undue importance on some pieces of information rather than others. For example, we tend to value information that comes to mind quickly and to discount any additional facts. We also tend to place greater emphasis on information that confirms our existing beliefs.

Before meditation
Ordinarily, some people may find it difficult to control their thoughts and emotions. These can become negative, which can lead to anxiety or depression.

SPIRITUAL EXERCISE

The practice of meditation is rooted in religious traditions, particularly those of ancient India and China, and in the mid-20th century, scientists began to study its benefits. In the 1970s, Jon Kabat-Zinn proposed that, even outside religious contexts, meditation helps people let go of obsessive thoughts and emotions and feel less stressed. Some people use meditation to foster mindfulness: a state in which we detach from our thoughts and feelings and simply observe them coming and going in our minds. Many people find this state helpful in alleviating anxiety and depression.

During meditation
When we meditate, we can practice freeing ourselves from our thoughts and emotions and examine them from a detached viewpoint.

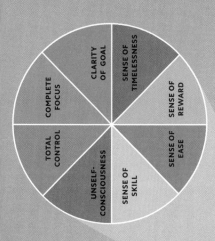

CLARITY OF GOAL

SENSE OF TIMELESSNESS

COMPLETE FOCUS

SENSE OF REWARD

TOTAL CONTROL

SENSE OF EASE

UNSELF-CONSCIOUSNESS

SENSE OF SKILL

IN THE ZONE

In 1975, Mihaly Csikszentmihalyi observed that when we devote a lot of time to an activity that demands our complete concentration, we often enter into what he called the "flow" state. This is a state of mind in which we lose all sense of self and time and are no longer conscious of the processes involved in carrying out a particular task. Csikszentmihalyi noticed that we only achieve flow when we use specific skills to reach an achievable but challenging goal—whether that be playing a musical instrument, exercising, or gardening.

> "Flow: a state in which people are so involved in an activity that nothing else seems to matter."
> Mihaly Csikszentmihalyi

BOREDOM

FLOW

ANXIETY

SKILL LEVEL

DIFFICULTY OF TASK

DISOR

AND

THERA

DERS
PIES

Psychology and neuroscience developed side by side, offering a greater understanding of the mind and the brain and a more nuanced view of mental health conditions. Early psychologists abandoned the practice of diagnosing people as either "sane" or "insane" and instead began cataloging the symptoms associated with psychological problems, eventually developing the modern system for classifying psychological disorders (see pp.108–109). Some of these problems can be treated medically by specialist doctors known as psychiatrists. Others can be treated by clinical psychologists using a range of therapies (see pp.126–127).

DIAGNOSING DISORDERS

When diagnosing psychological disorders, psychologists and psychiatrists rely on their clinical training and experience. They may also refer to either the World Health Organization's *International Classification of Disease* (ICD-11) or the American Psychiatric Association's *Diagnostic and Statistical Manual of Mental Disorders* (DSM-5), which describe and classify different disorders. Here is a selection of common classifications according to the DSM-5.

NEURODEVELOPMENTAL DISORDERS
Developmental challenges that begin early in a child's life

- **AUTISM SPECTRUM DISORDER (ASD)** (see p.110)
- **ATTENTION-DEFICIT/HYPERACTIVITY DISORDER (ADHD)** (see p.111)
- **SPECIFIC LEARNING DISORDER**
Having difficulties acquiring certain academic skills, such as doing mathematics

SCHIZOPHRENIA SPECTRUM & OTHER PSYCHOTIC DISORDERS
Characterized by hallucinations, delusions, disorganized thinking, and unusual behavior

- **DELUSIONAL DISORDER**
Having fixed beliefs about oneself and one's environment, both positive and negative, that are untrue
- **SCHIZOPHRENIA** (see p.112)

BIPOLAR & RELATED DISORDERS
Fluctuations over time between mania and depression

- **BIPOLAR I DISORDER** (see p.113)
- **BIPOLAR II DISORDER** (see p.113)
- **CYCLOTHYMIC DISORDER** (see p.113)

DEPRESSIVE DISORDERS
Having sad, empty, or irritable moods that are persistent and uncharacteristic

- **MAJOR DEPRESSIVE DISORDER** (see p.114)
- **DYSTHYMIA**
Mild depression lasting at least two years

ANXIETY DISORDERS
Extreme levels of fear and anxiety that make it difficult for a person to function at their best

GENERALIZED ANXIETY DISORDER (GAD)
(see p.116)

PANIC DISORDER
(see p.116)

PHOBIAS (see p.117)

OBSESSIVE COMPULSIVE & RELATED DISORDERS
Obsessive thoughts, often followed by compulsive behaviors that only temporarily reduce anxiety

OBSESSIVE COMPULSIVE DISORDER (OCD)
(see p.118)

BODY DYSMORPHIC DISORDER (BDD)
(see p.119)

TRAUMA- & STRESSOR-RELATED DISORDERS
Stress and anxiety caused by exposure to traumatic events

REACTIVE ATTACHMENT DISORDER
Emotional and behavioral withdrawal shown by children under the age of 5

POSTTRAUMATIC STRESS DISORDER (PTSD) (see p.120)

ADJUSTMENT DISORDERS
Impairment of function within three months of experiencing a traumatic event

DISSOCIATIVE DISORDERS
A lack of integration between awareness, thoughts, feelings, memory, identity, and behavior

DISSOCIATIVE IDENTITY DISORDER (DID)
(see p.121)

PICA
Eating substances that are not nutritious

FEEDING & EATING DISORDERS
Changes in a person's eating habits that are detrimental to their health and well-being

ANOREXIA NERVOSA (see p.122)

BULIMIA NERVOSA (see p.122)

BINGE EATING DISORDER
(see p.122)

SUBSTANCE-RELATED & ADDICTIVE DISORDERS
Addiction to substances or activities that activate the brain's reward system in an unhealthy way

SUBSTANCE-RELATED DISORDERS
(see p.123)

GAMBLING DISORDER
(see p.123)

PERSONALITY DISORDERS
Patterns of feelings and behaviors that are very different from those expected by society

CLUSTER A (see pp.124–125)

CLUSTER B (see pp.124–125)

CLUSTER C (see pp.124–125)

PROCESSING DIFFERENTLY

Autism spectrum disorder (ASD) can impact the ways in which a person processes certain information and interacts with other people. Symptoms are specific to each individual but can range from not understanding social cues to avoiding eye contact or not being able to speak. Some autistic people may also display restricted, repetitive behaviors; be over- or undersensitive to sensory stimuli; have a limited range of interests; or struggle to adjust to new routines. ASD is usually diagnosed in children, but some individuals—particularly women or people who present as female—may remain undiagnosed until well into adulthood.

Ranges of impact

ASD impacts each person differently: an individual may experience little or no difficulty in some areas but serious difficulty in others.

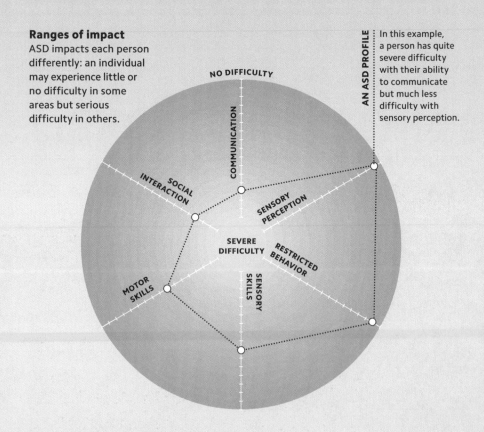

AN ASD PROFILE In this example, a person has quite severe difficulty with their ability to communicate but much less difficulty with sensory perception.

NO DIFFICULTY

COMMUNICATION

SOCIAL INTERACTION

SENSORY PERCEPTION

SEVERE DIFFICULTY

RESTRICTED BEHAVIOR

MOTOR SKILLS

SENSORY SKILLS

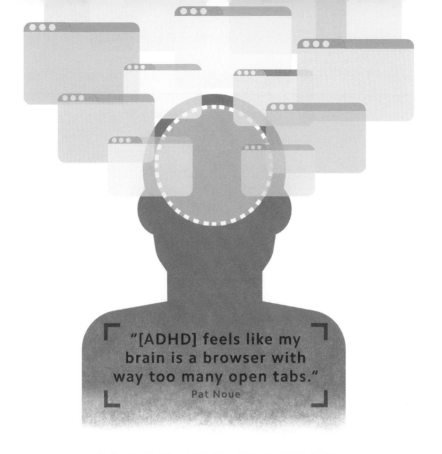

"[ADHD] feels like my brain is a browser with way too many open tabs."
Pat Noue

HARD TO FOCUS

Attention deficit hyperactivity disorder (ADHD) can be characterized by a tendency for a person focus intensely on certain tasks but struggle to concentrate on less stimulating activities, such as chores. A person with ADHD may have difficulty making plans, interrupt conversations, or appear careless or forgetful. They may also be impulsive or talkative and may need to move around or fidget in order to concentrate. Based on current guidelines, whatever a person's age, they have to have shown symptoms in more than one setting (such as at school and at home) before the age of 12 in order to be diagnosed with ADHD.

DELUSIONS, PARANOIA, AND ALTERED THINKING

A person with schizophrenia does not always know what is real and what is not real. They may hear voices; see, smell, or touch things that are not there (hallucinations); or have strong beliefs that are untrue (delusions). This can make it very difficult to function on a daily basis. Psychologists classify the symptoms of schizophrenia as either "positive" (additions to a person's mental state that change the way they think or behave) or "negative" (the absence of behaviors, thoughts, or abilities that are found in a healthy person). Individuals with schizophrenia can still live fruitful and fulfilling lives, particularly by working with a treatment plan that is appropriate for them.

POSITIVE SYMPTOMS

HALLUCINATIONS

DELUSIONS

SENSATIONS THAT ARE NOT REAL

UNIDENTIFIED SMELLS AND TASTES

FEELINGS OF BEING CONTROLLED

HEARING VOICES

NEGATIVE SYMPTOMS

DIFFICULTY COMMUNICATING

DISORGANIZED THOUGHTS

"FLATTENED" EMOTIONS

LACK OF WILLPOWER OR MOTIVATION

SLOW MOVEMENTS

WITHDRAWAL

TIREDNESS

HIGHS AND LOWS

EXTREME

Bipolar disorder is characterized by fluctuations between high mood (mania) and low mood (depression). During a manic episode, a person may feel invincible, sleep little, talk a lot, and act impulsively. In contrast, during a depressive episode, they generally suffer symptoms of depression (see p.114). Both kinds of episode can also involve delusions or hallucinations (see opposite) and can put the person at risk of harm. There are three types of bipolar disorder: bipolar I, bipolar II, and cyclothymia.

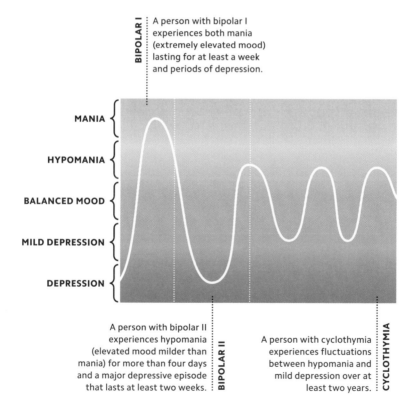

BIPOLAR I

A person with bipolar I experiences both mania (extremely elevated mood) lasting for at least a week and periods of depression.

MANIA

HYPOMANIA

BALANCED MOOD

MILD DEPRESSION

DEPRESSION

BIPOLAR II

A person with bipolar II experiences hypomania (elevated mood milder than mania) for more than four days and a major depressive episode that lasts at least two weeks.

CYCLOTHYMIA

A person with cyclothymia experiences fluctuations between hypomania and mild depression over at least two years.

A DARK CLOUD

The symptoms of depression are wide-ranging—from low self-esteem, negative thinking, and decreased motivation, to changes in sleep patterns, fatigue, and changes in appetite. A person with depression may also have low energy, feel guilty or worthless, or have difficulty concentrating. Extreme cases can involve having suicidal thoughts. Depression manifests in different ways: some people cry, whereas others may feel irritable, achy, or overwhelmed. Some describe feeling as if they are carrying a heavy weight, are moving through molasses, or have a dark cloud hanging over them. Psychologists diagnose depression when a person has shown symptoms for at least two weeks and has lost interest in activities they used to enjoy.

DISTORTED REALITY

Some new parents may experience symptoms of depression, and some may have thoughts of harm coming to their baby—or even of causing it (although they never would in reality). Such thoughts are accompanied by feelings of guilt and shame.

PREGNANCY, PARENTHOOD, AND MENTAL HEALTH

Many people experience mood changes (sometimes called "baby blues") during or after pregnancy. Perinatal mental illness is different, however: changes are longer term and more severe. During pregnancy or up to a year after birth, parents may experience various symptoms that psychologists would associate with mental illness, including depression (see opposite), severe anxiety, or panic attacks (see p.116). Some may also develop obsessive-compulsive symptoms (see p.118) or psychotic thinking (see p.108).

FEARING THE WORST

People with anxiety disorders have intense and prolonged feelings of fear and unease, often in everyday circumstances. Generalized anxiety disorder (GAD) is diagnosed if their anxiety affects their functioning, occurs more days than not, and lasts for at least six months. A related condition is panic disorder, in which a person has sudden, isolated attacks of panic or fear. Both disorders involve excessive fear of facing a real or imagined threat. Fear activates our autonomic nervous system (see pp.42–43), which readies us to fight, flee, or freeze when faced with danger. This results in the physical symptoms of anxiety and panic attacks.

MENTAL SYMPTOMS

Anxiety can disrupt sleep and impair concentration. Panic attacks can make a person feel that they are dying, having a heart attack, or "going insane."

PHYSICAL SYMPTOMS

Anxiety can lead to muscle tension, restlessness, or fatigue, while panic attacks involve shortness of breath, an increased heart rate, feelings of choking, or discomfort in the chest or stomach.

DEBILITATING FEAR

A specific phobia is an irrational but persistent fear triggered by a particular thing, such as an object or a situation. A person may develop a specific phobia after a traumatic event. Triggers for specific phobias fall into five categories: animal (such as spiders), natural environment (such as heights), blood-injection-injury (such as injections), situational (such as plane journeys), and unique others (such as loud noises, certain foods, or clowns). Complex phobias, such as agoraphobia (fear of being in situations that might be difficult to escape, such as crowded spaces) or social phobia (fear of being in social situations), can have a more disruptive effect on a person's life, because the person may avoid people or particular places.

INTENSE FEAR
When encountered, the thing triggers an exaggerated feeling of fear or sense of danger—leading to extreme anxiety or a panic attack.

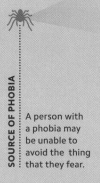

SOURCE OF PHOBIA
A person with a phobia may be unable to avoid the thing that they fear.

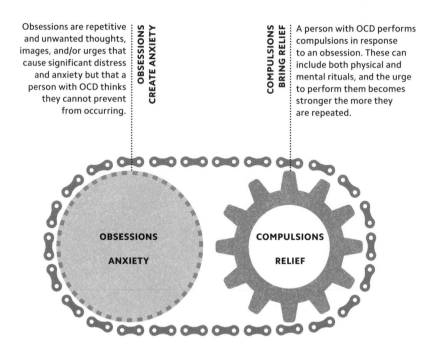

Obsessions are repetitive and unwanted thoughts, images, and/or urges that cause significant distress and anxiety but that a person with OCD thinks they cannot prevent from occurring.

OBSESSIONS CREATE ANXIETY

COMPULSIONS BRING RELIEF

A person with OCD performs compulsions in response to an obsession. These can include both physical and mental rituals, and the urge to perform them becomes stronger the more they are repeated.

OBSESSIONS

ANXIETY

COMPULSIONS

RELIEF

INTRUSIVE THOUGHTS AND REPETITIVE URGES

Obsessive compulsive disorder (OCD) involves cycles of unwanted thoughts and compulsive behaviors. People with OCD experience intrusive and disturbing thought patterns (or "obsessions"), which can cause them great anxiety. Performing repetitive behaviors (or "compulsions"), such as counting, washing, or repeating a phrase in their head, can reduce the person's feelings of anxiety—but only temporarily. Both obsessions and compulsions can disrupt an individual's day-to-day life.

Negative reflections
When a person has BDD, their self-image—that is, how they perceive themselves—is distorted, or does not reflect reality.

DISTORTED SELF-IMAGE

Body dysmorphic disorder (BDD) causes a person to worry or obsess about a feature of their body that they perceive to be a flaw but that is invisible or barely noticeable to others. The person may feel that other people are judging them on this feature, which may cause them great distress and lead them to obsessively check it and try to conceal it. Such repetitive thoughts and behaviors can become uncontrollable and make it difficult for the person to engage in everyday activities.

AFTERMATH OF TRAUMA

People may develop posttraumatic stress disorder (PTSD) as a result of experiencing or witnessing a distressing or life-threatening event. A person with PTSD may experience prolonged hypervigilance: that is, being constantly on high alert in anticipation of further danger. They may also undergo flashbacks (vivid memories of the event), panic attacks, insomnia, or nightmares; have difficulty concentrating; or feel irritable. Symptoms usually appear within a few weeks of the traumatic event and can be long-lasting. PTSD can make people vulnerable to other mental health problems and to self-destructive attempts to cope, such as alcohol or drug abuse.

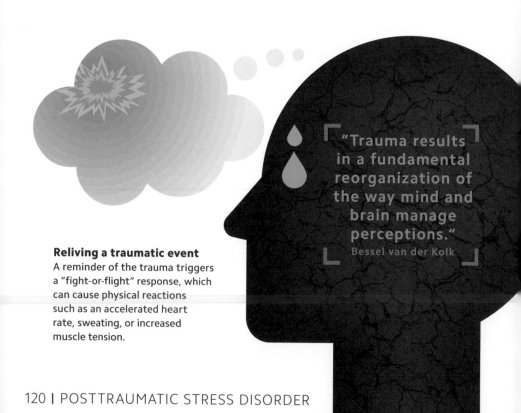

"Trauma results in a fundamental reorganization of the way mind and brain manage perceptions."
Bessel van der Kolk

Reliving a traumatic event
A reminder of the trauma triggers a "fight-or-flight" response, which can cause physical reactions such as an accelerated heart rate, sweating, or increased muscle tension.

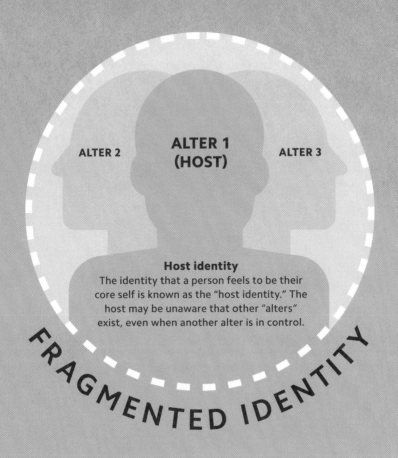

ALTER 2

ALTER 1 (HOST)

ALTER 3

Host identity
The identity that a person feels to be their core self is known as the "host identity." The host may be unaware that other "alters" exist, even when another alter is in control.

FRAGMENTED IDENTITY

When a person has to cope with extreme trauma that lasts for an extended period of time, they may develop a condition known as dissociative identity disorder (DID). This is a complex form of dissociation (feeling detached from reality) in which the person's identity is divided into two or more different parts, or "alters." Alters might seem to be different genders or ages; have distinct thoughts, feelings, and memories; or speak different languages. Each alter may take control of the person's thoughts and behavior intermittently. Disconnection between the alters can result in blanks or gaps in memory, which can cause significant distress and difficulties with daily life.

Anorexia nervosa
This disorder involves trying to avoid weight gain, often (but not always) by eating much less than the body needs—typically due to fear of gaining weight.

Bulimia nervosa
This disorder involves a cycle between eating large amounts (binging), then emptying (purging) the stomach in an attempt to avoid weight gain.

Binge eating disorder
This disorder involves regularly eating large amounts in a short period of time (binging), often despite feeling ashamed, disgusted, or out of control.

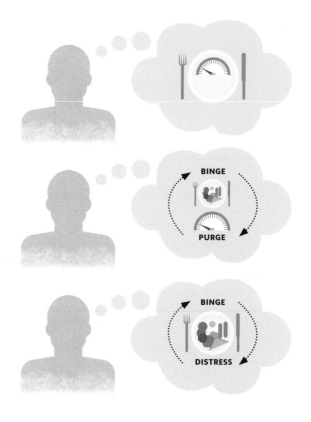

PROBLEMS WITH EATING

Eating disorders are changes in a person's eating-related behaviors that are harmful to their health, and are characterized by a reliance on managing eating patterns, often as a way of coping or feeling in control. They can develop for a number of reasons, such as having experienced traumatic events or having difficulty expressing emotions. The person may feel afraid of gaining weight or ashamed of eating food but may find it very difficult to change their behavior. Eating disorders can have serious physical effects, as well as mental and emotional ones, and may be life-threatening if left untreated.

COMPULSION/ACTION

PLEASURE/RELIEF

Someone with an addiction is unable to stop repeating a particular behavior (such as using drugs, gambling, drinking, or simply looking at their smartphone), even though they know that it is harming them. This is because physical changes in the person's brain prompt them to repeat the behavior. If the person is unable to overcome their addiction, they may go to dangerous lengths to satisfy it. If they manage to stop, they may relapse after a painful period of withdrawal. However, rehabilitation programs and social support can help individuals with a particular addiction to escape its dangerous cycle.

TENSION/NEED

REGRET/GUILT

STRUGGLING TO RESIST

CLUSTER A

Schizoid personality disorder
Symptoms can include: lack of interest in other people; preferring to be alone; limited range of emotional expression; difficulty enjoying most activities and/or recognizing "normal" social cues.

Paranoid personality disorder
Symptoms can include: distrust of others and their motives; difficulty confiding in others for fear of being betrayed; belief that nonthreatening situations are dangerous; tendency to hold grudges.

Schizotypal personality disorder
Symptoms can include: peculiar thinking, speech, or behavior; mild perceptual distortions; social anxiety; suspiciousness; "inappropriate" emotional responses; difficulty forming close relationships.

RELATING DIFFERENTLY

People with personality disorders display fixed patterns of behavior and thinking that differ from society's norms, leading to problems with social functioning. Psychologists group the disorders into three clusters based on shared characteristics. Cluster A symptoms include "odd" or "eccentric" behavior; Cluster B symptoms include "dramatic," "emotional," or "erratic" behavior; and Cluster C symptoms include "anxious" or "fearful" behavior.

CLUSTER B

Antisocial personality disorder
Symptoms can include: disregard for the needs or feelings of others; persistent lying and stealing; impulsive, aggressive behavior; lack of remorse; disregard for the safety of others and oneself.

Borderline personality disorder
Symptoms can include: unstable self-image and relationships; fear of being alone; mood swings; feeling empty; recurrent anger or paranoia; impulsive or risky behavior; suicidal thoughts.

Histrionic personality disorder
Symptoms can include: persistently seeking attention; very emotional or dramatic behavior; strong opinions based on little evidence; vulnerability to influence from others; excessive concern with physical appearance.

Narcissistic personality disorder
Symptoms can include: feeling more important than others; fantasizing about being powerful, successful, or attractive; exaggerating achievements; expecting praise and admiration; feeling envious.

CLUSTER C

Avoidant personality disorder
Symptoms can include: being socially withdrawn; feeling inadequate; being very sensitive to criticism or rejection; extreme shyness; avoiding new situations or people; fear of disapproval or ridicule.

Obsessive compulsive personality disorder
Symptoms can include: preoccupation with details and orderliness; trying to control situations or other people; difficulty delegating tasks or completing projects due to having strict standards.

Dependent personality disorder
Symptoms can include: feeling the need to be taken care of; lack of confidence; constant need for advice; tolerating abusive treatment; difficulty disagreeing with others; fear of disapproval; fear of abandonment.

TREATING DISORDERS

When treating patients, most mental health professionals choose one of several general approaches, and within each approach they may specialize in a specific type of therapy. The majority of these, known as "talking therapies," involve an expert therapist communicating regularly with the patient either face-to-face or online. Here are five of the major approaches and some of the most common types of therapy associated with them.

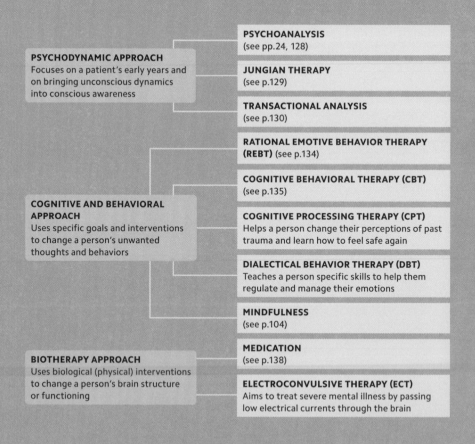

PSYCHODYNAMIC APPROACH
Focuses on a patient's early years and on bringing unconscious dynamics into conscious awareness

PSYCHOANALYSIS
(see pp.24, 128)

JUNGIAN THERAPY
(see p.129)

TRANSACTIONAL ANALYSIS
(see p.130)

COGNITIVE AND BEHAVIORAL APPROACH
Uses specific goals and interventions to change a person's unwanted thoughts and behaviors

RATIONAL EMOTIVE BEHAVIOR THERAPY (REBT) (see p.134)

COGNITIVE BEHAVIORAL THERAPY (CBT)
(see p.135)

COGNITIVE PROCESSING THERAPY (CPT)
Helps a person change their perceptions of past trauma and learn how to feel safe again

DIALECTICAL BEHAVIOR THERAPY (DBT)
Teaches a person specific skills to help them regulate and manage their emotions

MINDFULNESS
(see p.104)

BIOTHERAPY APPROACH
Uses biological (physical) interventions to change a person's brain structure or functioning

MEDICATION
(see p.138)

ELECTROCONVULSIVE THERAPY (ECT)
Aims to treat severe mental illness by passing low electrical currents through the brain

PERSON-CENTERED THERAPY
(see p.131)

GESTALT THERAPY
(see p.132)

EXISTENTIAL THERAPY
(see p.133)

EMOTION-FOCUSED THERAPY (EFT)
Helps a person better understand, accept, and regulate their emotions

SOLUTION-FOCUSED BRIEF THERAPY (SFBT)
Encourages a person to set themselves specific, achievable, and measurable goals

HUMANISTIC APPROACH
Encourages a person to know and accept themselves fully so that they can fulfill their potential

SOMATIC THERAPY
Uses body-centered techniques, such as yoga, to relieve tension and restore mental balance

EYE MOVEMENT DESENSITIZATION AND REPROCESSING (EMDR) (see p.137)

HYPNOTHERAPY
Places a person in a trancelike state, in which their mind is more receptive to change

ARTS-BASED THERAPY
Promotes self-expression and mental well-being through art and music

ANIMAL-ASSISTED THERAPY
Uses the bond between humans and animals to boost a person's mood and self-esteem

FAMILY SYSTEMS THERAPY
(see p.136)

SYSTEMIC APPROACH
Seeks to help a person within the context of their family or another close relationship rather than individually

CONTEXTUAL THERAPY
Encourages family members to recognize each others' emotional needs

DYADIC DEVELOPMENTAL THERAPY
Helps children who have suffered emotional trauma bond with their caregivers

Dream analysis
Analyzing a client's dreams can provide insights into problems that the client may not be consciously aware of.

Transference
How the client relates to and feels about their analyst may indicate how they relate to other people.

Free association
The analyst encourages the client to speak as openly as possible without censoring themselves. This enables their unconscious thoughts and feelings to emerge.

Freudian slips
The client may pause unnecessarily or use an inappropriate word. Such anomalies, known as "Freudian slips," may suggest that there is a link between certain words and unconscious thoughts.

UNCOVERING THE PAST

Based on psychoanalysis (see p.24), psychodynamic therapy uses a number of techniques (see above) to retrieve childhood memories and feelings from the client's unconscious mind so that they can become aware of them. The analyst listens closely to the client but reveals very little about themselves. As a result, the client often redirects their feelings about other people onto the analyst, in a process called "transference." Using "countertransference," the analyst then interprets their own feelings toward the client in order to gain insight into the nature of the client's difficulties.

BALANCING THE SOUL

According to Carl Jung (see p.28), psychological disorders develop
when the parts of a person's self are not in balance. These parts
include: the persona (the side of ourselves that we present to the
world), the shadow (the side of ourselves that we do not like), and the
anima or animus (the "female" element in men and the "male" element
in women). Jung also believed that our conscious minds are rooted in
the "collective unconscious"—a store of mental patterns that are
common to all humans. Jungian therapy attempts to bring all of these
parts into balance, enabling the client to find their "true self."

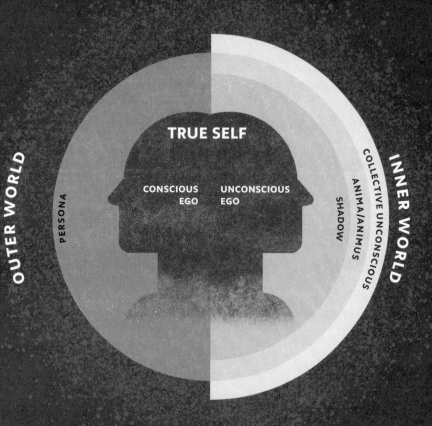

OUTER WORLD

TRUE SELF

CONSCIOUS
EGO

UNCONSCIOUS
EGO

PERSONA

SHADOW

ANIMA/ANIMUS

COLLECTIVE UNCONSCIOUS

INNER WORLD

PARENT, ADULT, CHILD

Created by Eric Berne in the 1960s, transactional analysis (TA) is based on the idea that, as adults, our personalities are made up of three "ego states": "Parent," "Adult," and "Child." TA analysts hold that we can have a "transaction" (interaction) with another person using any of these states. They help their clients interact with others using the "Adult" state (in which they are in control of themselves and grounded in the present) instead of the "Child" state (acting based on how they felt as a child) or the "Parent" state (copying how their parents used to behave).

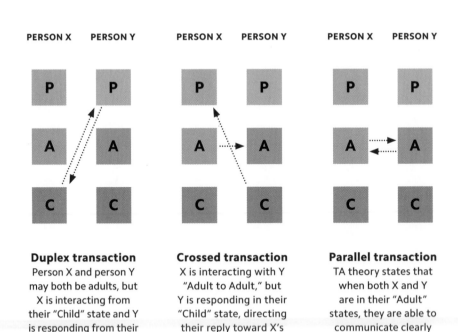

Duplex transaction
Person X and person Y may both be adults, but X is interacting from their "Child" state and Y is responding from their "Parent" state.

Crossed transaction
X is interacting with Y "Adult to Adult," but Y is responding in their "Child" state, directing their reply toward X's "Parent" state.

Parallel transaction
TA theory states that when both X and Y are in their "Adult" states, they are able to communicate clearly and logically.

LED BY THE CLIENT

Carl Rogers developed person-centered therapy (also known as client-centered or Rogerian therapy) in the 1950s. Therapists who use this approach treat their clients as equals and show them "unconditional positive regard" (see p.39). Each client decides what they would like to work on based on their own personal values and progresses at their own pace toward mutually agreed goals. By building a trusting relationship with the client, the therapist helps them attain their full potential.

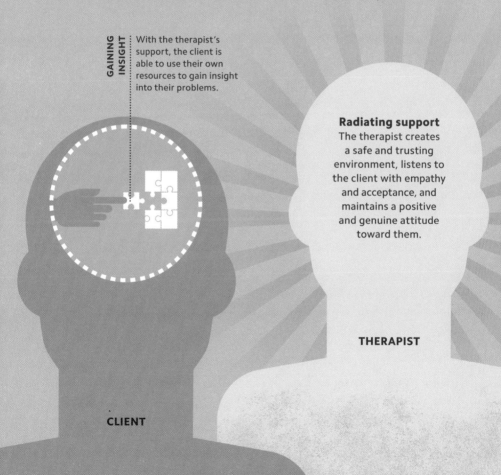

GAINING INSIGHT
With the therapist's support, the client is able to use their own resources to gain insight into their problems.

Radiating support
The therapist creates a safe and trusting environment, listens to the client with empathy and acceptance, and maintains a positive and genuine attitude toward them.

THERAPIST

CLIENT

According to Perls, this outer layer indicates the fake and inauthentic way a person presents themselves, concealing their true self.

PHONY

PHOBIC

Perls described this second layer as one where a person fears seeing who they really are, so they cover up any vulnerabilities.

In this third layer, a person is "stuck": lacking a sense of direction and unable to make decisions.

IMPASSE

IMPLOSIVE

In the fourth layer, a person confronts their vulnerabilities, or "deadness."

EXPLOSIVE

In the fifth and final layer, a person reaches "catharsis," in which they encounter their true, deep feelings—such as joy or grief.

THE WHOLE PERSON

Fritz and Laura Perls established Gestalt therapy in the 1940s. Gestalt therapists focus on the "whole picture" and on their relationship with their clients "in the here and now." They encourage clients to develop an increased awareness of themselves by paying attention to perceptions and feelings rather than by interpreting past events. Fritz Perls proposed that, in order to achieve full self-awareness, clients need to work through five "layers of neurosis": phony, phobic, impasse, implosive, and explosive.

Existential therapy helps a person explore their challenges from a philosophical perspective. It centers around the idea that we lead more fulfilling lives if we accept that we cannot change the limitations of our existence (such as that we are ultimately alone or that we cannot escape death). Existential therapists adopt a direct, honest, and confrontative attitude. They encourage clients to pursue self-awareness; identify their own values, purpose, and sense of meaning; recognize which parts of their lives they can control; and accept responsibility for the choices they make.

Before therapy
A person may feel overwhelmed with anxiety about life. They may experience feelings of loneliness and depression.

After therapy
A person accepts life's challenges and limitations and pursues meaning and joy by taking responsibility for their actions.

CONFRONTING EXISTENCE

| FREEDOM |
| ISOLATION |
| MORTALITY |
| MEANINGLESSNESS |

| FREEDOM |
| ISOLATION |
| MORTALITY |
| MEANINGLESSNESS |

RESPONSIBILITY

HEALING REASON

Introduced by Albert Ellis in 1955, rational emotive behavior therapy (REBT) is an early form of cognitive behavioral therapy (CBT, see opposite) that deals with the distress caused by "irrational" beliefs: that is, beliefs that distort reality or lead to self-defeating behavior. REBT uses the "ABC" model to identify three aspects of a person's distress: an "activating event" (A); their "belief" about that event (B); and their emotional response, or the "consequence" (C). REBT therapists focus on helping individuals identify irrational beliefs they hold about themselves and develop unconditional self-acceptance.

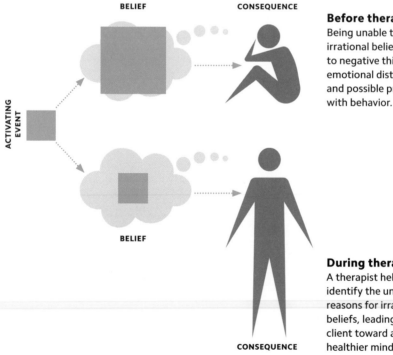

Before therapy
Being unable to control irrational beliefs leads to negative thinking, emotional distress, and possible problems with behavior.

During therapy
A therapist helps identify the underlying reasons for irrational beliefs, leading the client toward a healthier mindset.

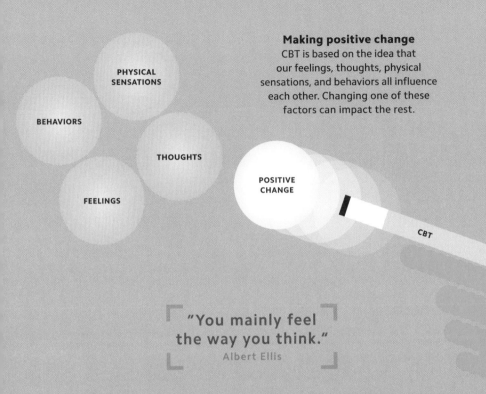

Making positive change
CBT is based on the idea that our feelings, thoughts, physical sensations, and behaviors all influence each other. Changing one of these factors can impact the rest.

PHYSICAL SENSATIONS

BEHAVIORS

THOUGHTS

POSITIVE CHANGE

FEELINGS

CBT

"You mainly feel
the way you think."
Albert Ellis

CHANGING PATTERNS

Based on the work of Albert Ellis (see opposite) and Aaron Beck in the 1960s, cognitive behavioral therapy (CBT) focuses on changing patterns of thinking or behavior that have a negative impact on an individual's well-being. CBT therapists help their clients see that it is their perception of an event that is causing emotional problems, not the event itself. They encourage clients to identify "cognitive distortions" (forms of negative thinking) or negative behaviors, challenge them, and replace them with more realistic and positive thoughts or behaviors. In turn, this can lead to improvements in mood and physical symptoms.

> **"That which is created in a relationship can be fixed in a relationship."**
> Murray Bowen

GROUP DYNAMICS

Murray Bowen developed family systems therapy in the 1950s. He argued that every family is an emotional unit and believed that if one person in a family changes emotionally, then that will influence emotional changes in the others. In therapy, clients gain insight into current and past family relationships using a chart called a "genogram" and learn how to establish good communication, problem-solve, and set boundaries.

  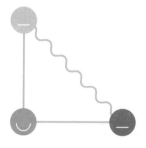 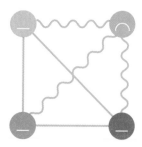

Two in conflict
If conflict arises between two people, they may seek therapy in order to help them communicate more directly and effectively, reducing stress.

Emotional triangle
Two people in conflict may put a third person between them to avoid relating to each other; family therapy can help resolve this.

Family of four
In larger families, therapy can help improve stressful relationships between two parents or between parents and their children.

Bilateral stimulation
The therapist directs the client's
eye movement from side to side.
This stimulates processing systems
in the client's brain that may have
become "stuck" due to trauma.

FACING TRAUMA

Devised by Francine Shapiro in the 1980s, eye movement
desensitization and reprocessing (EMDR) aims to benefit people
who have experienced traumatic events. It involves a technique
called "bilateral stimulation," in which the therapist moves a
finger back and forth while the client follows it with their eyes.
At the same time, the client briefly focuses on a traumatic
memory. The eye movements are thought to help the client's
brain "process" the trauma properly, enabling them to heal.

Focus on trauma
The client focuses on a traumatic
memory while moving their eyes.
This helps their brain to process the
trauma like an ordinary memory,
lessening its impact.

TREATING THE BODY

The medications used for treating psychological disorders alter the chemistry of patients' brains to help them become healthier. Cells in our brains exchange signals via chemicals known as "neurotransmitters" (see pp.42–43), and different medications either enhance or reduce one or more of these signals. For example, an antidepressant may enhance the neurotransmitter serotonin, which regulates mood.

PRESCRIPTION

MEDICATION CATEGORY:	FOR PEOPLE DIAGNOSED WITH:	EFFECTS:
Antidepressants	Depression Low mood	Decrease depressive symptoms; increase positive thinking and improve mood
Antipsychotics	Bipolar disorder Schizophrenia	Decrease hallucinations, delusions, and negative behaviors
Anti-anxiety drugs	Anxiety disorders PTSD	Decrease worry, reactivity, and muscle tension; increase calmness and relaxation
Mood stabilizers	Bipolar disorder Mood disorders	Decrease mania and depression; balance mood; increase calm and sense of control
Stimulants	ADHD	Decrease restlessness; increase concentration and motivation

The path of life
According to R. D. Laing, mental illnesses are natural reactions to the difficulties that people encounter on the "path of life." He argued that, under certain circumstances, it is sane for people to behave "insanely."

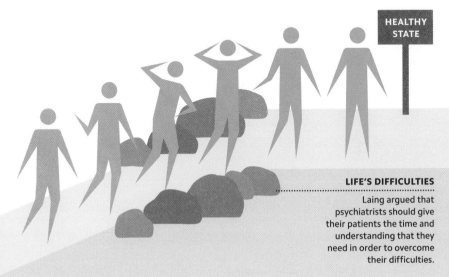

HEALTHY STATE

LIFE'S DIFFICULTIES
Laing argued that psychiatrists should give their patients the time and understanding that they need in order to overcome their difficulties.

NATURAL REACTIONS

The antipsychiatry movement started in the 1960s, in opposition to various psychiatric practices, including that of detaining people in asylums. Its supporters also criticized the use of various forms of brain surgery, which, they argued, damaged people for the sake of making them docile. R. D. Laing, a key (though controversial) figure in the movement, believed that most mental illnesses are in fact natural reactions that people have in intolerably stressful situations. He claimed that even severe symptoms, such as psychosis (see p.108), are part of the process of moving past difficult circumstances and toward a healthy state.

IDENT

AND

DIFFE

I T Y

R E N C E

In contrast to social psychologists (see pp.66–85), researchers studying the psychology of difference set out to identify and examine the specific characteristics that distinguish us as individuals. Initially, their work focused on intelligence, which is to some extent measurable (unlike, for example, personality). However, as the field developed, it became clear that there are many different kinds of intelligence. Similarly, psychologists abandoned the practice of classifying personalities as either "introverted" or "extroverted" and introduced a new system based on a wider range of personality traits and characteristics.

CARDINAL TRAITS

These traits dominate
and tend to define an
individual, such as
being altruistic or
Machiavellian.

"Personality is
less a finished
product than
a transitive
process."
Gordon Allport

SECONDARY TRAITS

These traits are only
expressed in specific
situations, such as
acting defensively
when under pressure.

CENTRAL TRAITS

These are generalized
characteristics that
describe a person's
basic personality, such
as being shy or clever.

HUMAN CHARACTERISTICS

First developed by Gordon Allport in the 1930s, trait theory
suggests that personality is made up of specific characteristics,
or "traits," which are a culmination of patterns of behavior,
thoughts, and emotions. Traits are expressed to varying
degrees but remain consistent over time, and trait theorists
focus on identifying and measuring them. Allport organized
these traits into a three-tiered hierarchy: cardinal traits,
central traits, and secondary traits. He argued that our
personalities are determined by genetics but can be influenced
by our environment, making them unique to each individual.

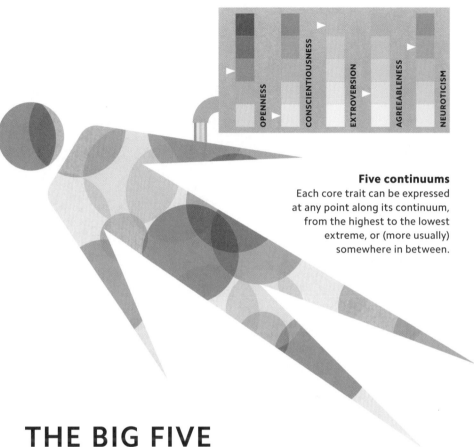

OPENNESS

CONSCIENTIOUSNESS

EXTROVERSION

AGREEABLENESS

NEUROTICISM

Five continuums
Each core trait can be expressed
at any point along its continuum,
from the highest to the lowest
extreme, or (more usually)
somewhere in between.

THE BIG FIVE

Since the 1950s, personality psychologists have been refining a
model often known by the acronym "OCEAN." It proposes that an
individual's personality is made up of five broad traits. Openness is
our willingness to try new experiences. Conscientiousness is the
degree to which we can be organized and disciplined. Extroversion
refers to our sociability and assertiveness. Agreeableness is the
extent to which we connect with others. Neuroticism refers to
our ability to regulate emotions. All five OCEAN traits are evident
across different cultural, ethnic, age, and gender groups, but each
individual expresses their traits in a unique way.

"Psychic energy"

Extroversion
According to Jung, extroverts direct their energy toward the external world. They also feel energized by being around others.

Introversion
Jung theorized that introverts direct their energy toward their own internal world and find time alone less draining than socializing.

ENERGY SOURCES

Carl Jung (see p.28) was one of the pioneers of personality psychology, and he questioned why different people have different personality traits. Jung identified two main personality types, "introvert" and "extrovert," which he defined in terms of what he called "psychic energy." He argued that introverts direct this energy inward, and so are more reflective in nature, and prefer to keep to themselves. Conversely, he claimed that extroverts direct their energy outward, and so are more sociable, more accommodating, and more willing to try new experiences.

TESTING PERSONALITY

Psychologists use what are known as psychometric tests to measure a person's intelligence, attitudes, behavior, and personality. There are two main kinds of personality tests: objective tests, in which a person "self-reports" their answers to standardized questions; and projective tests, in which an examiner reports how a person reacts to ambiguous stimuli, such as a Rorschach inkblot (see p.27) and assesses their unconscious thoughts and emotions. Employers sometimes use objective personality tests to assess whether a potential employee is suitable for a role.

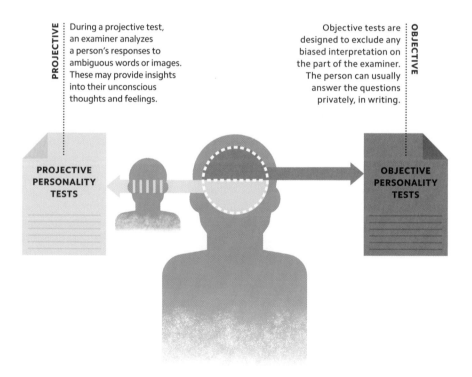

PROJECTIVE

During a projective test, an examiner analyzes a person's responses to ambiguous words or images. These may provide insights into their unconscious thoughts and feelings.

OBJECTIVE

Objective tests are designed to exclude any biased interpretation on the part of the examiner. The person can usually answer the questions privately, in writing.

PROJECTIVE PERSONALITY TESTS

OBJECTIVE PERSONALITY TESTS

FLUID AND CRYSTALLIZED

The Cattell–Horn theory was developed in the 1960s by Raymond Cattell and John Horn. They proposed that general intelligence has two aspects: fluid intelligence (logic) and crystallized intelligence (acquired knowledge). This theory provided a comprehensive basis for understanding cognition, and informs intelligence research today. However, a number of Cattell's more controversial beliefs have been widely criticized, such as his proposal that intelligence tests could be used to create an evolutionarily "superior" population by phasing out those of "lesser" intelligence, for example, through birth control.

Fluid intelligence
Cattell described this as the ability to think and problem-solve in an abstract way, independently of previous learning and experiences.

Crystallized intelligence
Cattell defined this as the ability to use previously acquired knowledge, building upon previous learnings and experiences.

General intelligence
Cattell considered overall intelligence and cognitive ability to be the culmination of both fluid and crystallized intelligence.

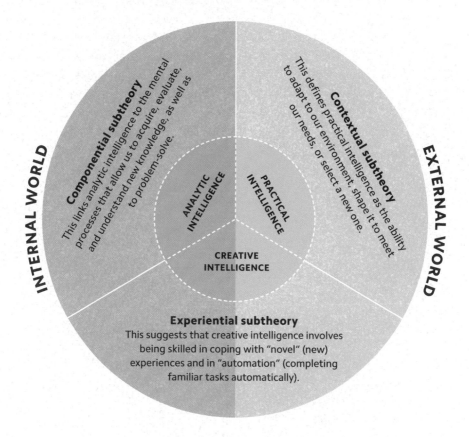

Componential subtheory
This links analytic intelligence to the mental processes that allow us to acquire, evaluate, and understand new knowledge, as well as to problem-solve.

Contextual subtheory
This defines practical intelligence as the ability to adapt to our environment, shape it to meet our needs, or select a new one.

ANALYTIC INTELLIGENCE

PRACTICAL INTELLIGENCE

CREATIVE INTELLIGENCE

Experiential subtheory
This suggests that creative intelligence involves being skilled in coping with "novel" (new) experiences and in "automation" (completing familiar tasks automatically).

INTERNAL WORLD

EXTERNAL WORLD

THREE INTELLIGENCES

In 1985, Robert Sternberg provided an alternative theory of intelligence to counter the Cattell–Horn theory (see opposite), which was based on psychometric testing (see p.145). Sternberg believed that intelligence is not defined solely by academic ability, but also includes our capacity to be creative and to adapt to our environment. He proposed that there are three types of intelligence: practical, creative, and analytic. Known as the triarchic theory of intelligence, Sternberg's model relies on three "subtheories," each of which relates to one of the three types of intelligence.

MEASURING CREATIVITY

In the 1960s, Ellis Paul Torrance developed a set of methods for testing a person's creativity, known as the Torrance Tests of Creative Thinking (TTCT). Torrance aimed to identify a set level of creativity (usually within children), but also to gain an understanding of that creativity in order to develop it further. The tests assess individuals by setting challenges using words or pictures, such as thinking of different uses for an object. They measure how flexible a person's responses are, as well as the range of ideas, originality, and detail that they supply.

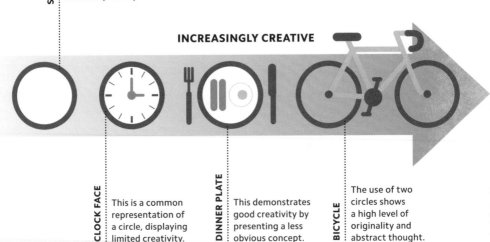

STIMULUS
In a picture test, a person is asked to embellish a given stimulus (a circle).

INCREASINGLY CREATIVE

CLOCK FACE
This is a common representation of a circle, displaying limited creativity.

DINNER PLATE
This demonstrates good creativity by presenting a less obvious concept.

BICYCLE
The use of two circles shows a high level of originality and abstract thought.

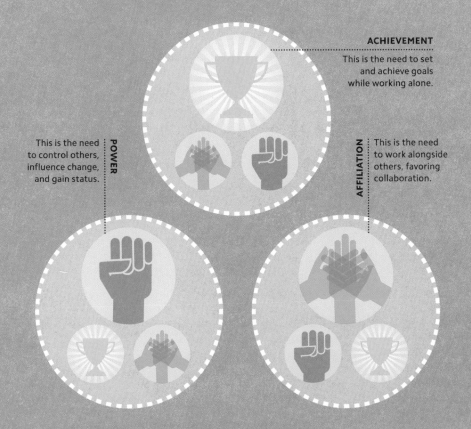

This is the need to set and achieve goals while working alone.

POWER
This is the need to control others, influence change, and gain status.

AFFILIATION
This is the need to work alongside others, favoring collaboration.

DRIVING MOTIVATORS

Building on the work of Abraham Maslow (see p.38) in the 1960s, David McClelland argued that people are motivated by three needs: achievement, power, and affiliation. He believed that each of these needs is present in all of us, irrespective of gender, race, age, or culture. However, he also suggested that needs are learned, and therefore that our dominant motivator depends on our individual cultures and life experiences. In workplace settings, managers sometimes use "need theory" to improve employees' performance by understanding what motivates them.

As we grow up, we start to gain an understanding of our identities: a coherent sense of who we are over time, reflected by patterns in our behavior and social interactions. In the 1960s, Erik Erikson argued that our identities begin to form during adolescence and that the process continues into old age (see pp.50–51). Many psychologists believe that personality is the foundation of identity, but that values, goals, and beliefs are also important—as are factors such as race, gender, disability, socioeconomic status, religion, and culture.

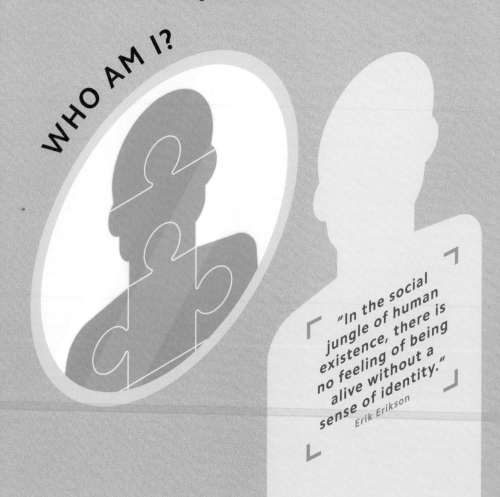

WHO AM I?

"In the social jungle of human existence, there is no feeling of being alive without a sense of identity."
Erik Erikson

Diffusion

Children in the first stage of identity formation have not explored or committed to an identity. They have yet to encounter role models.

Foreclosure

Some young adolescents may commit to an identity without exploring other options. This can continue until there are more role models and influences nearby.

NO EXPLORATION

NO COMMITMENT COMMITMENT

Moratorium

Many teenagers actively explore identity options without committing. They encounter new role models and question previously held and new beliefs.

EXPLORATION

Achievement

After encountering role models and exploring their options, an adolescent or young adult is ready to commit to their chosen identity.

FINDING AN IDENTITY

In 1966, James Marcia theorized that role models provide adolescents with examples of belief systems and ideologies. He proposed that we go through four progressive stages of identity development as we choose which beliefs to commit to (although not all adolescents go through every stage). Progression to a new stage may be triggered by a crisis, in which we reevaluate our beliefs and goals.

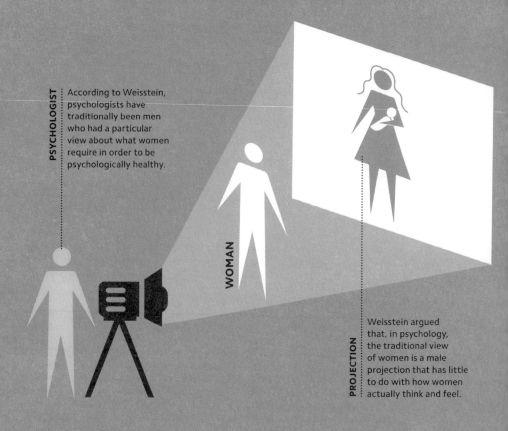

PSYCHOLOGIST

According to Weisstein, psychologists have traditionally been men who had a particular view about what women require in order to be psychologically healthy.

WOMAN

PROJECTION

Weisstein argued that, in psychology, the traditional view of women is a male projection that has little to do with how women actually think and feel.

MALE BIAS

In the 1970s, Naomi Weisstein raised important questions about how psychologists viewed women and their identities at the time. Weisstein argued that psychologists failed to acknowledge that a person's identity is not simply determined by their genes, but is also shaped by their environment, which may or may not encourage them to fulfill their true potential. She particularly challenged the Freudian approach (see pp.22–29), which presented women as being driven almost exclusively by the need to get married and raise children.

AFROCENTRIC PSYCHOLOGY

Linda James Myers conceived optimal psychology in the 1980s, in response to the mental health needs of African Americans. Myers argues that these needs are not always met by standard psychotherapies and that Western psychologists cannot help with many mental health problems because they fail to recognize that humans are fundamentally spiritual and communal beings. She proposes what she calls an "optimal" approach: encouraging individuals to embrace their own spiritual traditions—which they may have been unaware of or abandoned—and their interconnectedness with both nature and each other.

Optimal
For Myers, the "optimal" state of being is one in which we acknowledge that we are all connected—to each other, to nature, and to the divine.

Suboptimal
Myers proposed that the "suboptimal" state of being is one in which we see ourselves and the world as a set of individual, unrelated parts.

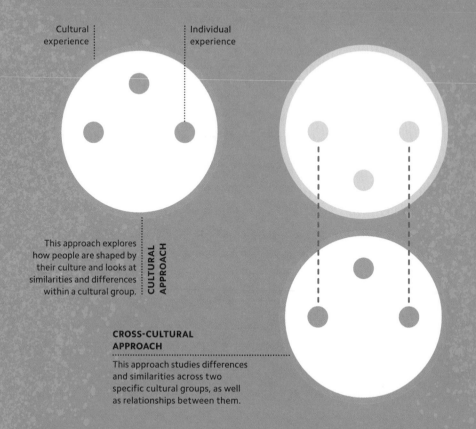

Cultural experience

Individual experience

This approach explores how people are shaped by their culture and looks at similarities and differences within a cultural group.

CULTURAL APPROACH

CROSS-CULTURAL APPROACH

This approach studies differences and similarities across two specific cultural groups, as well as relationships between them.

MINDS AND CULTURES

Multicultural psychologists study how cultural differences can influence the way that we function in society. They advocate the need to account for this influence in theory and research, arguing that it is vital to understand the psychology of both universal and culturally distinct human experiences. Sociocultural psychologists share this view, believing that our behavior and cognitive abilities are shaped by cultural influences. They claim that by taking these influences into account, psychologists will make their work more inclusive and representative of all communities.

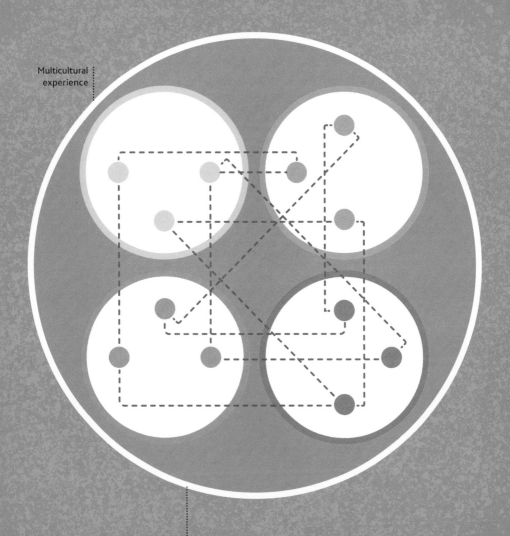

Multicultural
experience

MULTICULTURAL
APPROACH

This approach studies variables
such as race, religion, and
ethnicity. Researchers consider
differences and similarities
between many cultural
groups and how they relate
to one another.

"A culture-centered
perspective will
strengthen the
relevance and
applicability of
psychology."
Paul B. Pedersen

INDEX

Page numbers in **bold** refer to main entries.

A

abuse
  response to 57
  substance 109, 120, 123
acceptance 39, 131
achievement, as motivator
  149
addiction 109, **123**
Adler, Alfred 26
adolescence 47, 62, 150,
  151
affiliation, as motivator 149
African Americans 60, 153
agoraphobia 117
agreeableness 143
Ainsworth, Mary 56
alcohol abuse 120, 123
Allport, Gordon 80, 142
alters 121
analytic intelligence 147
anger 93
anima/animus 129
anorexia nervosa 109, **122**
antipsychiatry 139
antisocial behavior 57
antisocial personality
  disorder **125**
anxiety disorders 24, 94, 109,
  115, **116**, 118, 138
appetite 12
Armitage, George 94
Aronson, Elliot 61
Aronson's First Law **75**
Asch, Solomon 72
attachment theory 52, **54**
attention-deficit/
  hyperactivity disorder
  (ADHD) 108, **111**, 138
attention theory 87, **96**

Attitudes Toward Women
  Scale 81
authority figures **73**
autism
  autism spectrum disorder
    (ASD) 108, **110**
  sex and gender **65**
autonomic nervous system
  116
avoidant personality
  disorder **125**

B

Bandura, Albert 53
Baron-Cohen, Simon 65
Beck, Aaron 135
behavioral conditioning **33**,
  35
behaviorism **32–35**, 87
beliefs 23, 97, 103, 150, 151
  identifying irrational 134
Berne, Eric 130
bias 101, 103, 152
binge eating disorder 109,
  122
biopsychology **42–43**
bipolar disorder 15, 108,
  113, 138
body and mind **10**
body dysmorphic disorder
  (BDD) 109, **119**
borderline personality
  disorder (BPD) **125**
bottom-up processing **91**
Bowen, Murray 136
Bowlby, John 54
brain
  attention theory **96**
  biopsychology **42–43**

consciousness **89**
decision-making 102–103
information processing **94**,
  95, 96
male/female 65
pattern recognition **92**
perception **90–91**
physicalism 11
Broadbent, Donald 96
bulimia nervosa 109, **122**
bystander effect **77**

C

caregivers 50, 51, 52, 54,
  55, 56
Caspi, Avshalom 57
Cattell, Raymond 146
Cattell–Horn theory **146**, 147
cerebral cortex 42
change management 82
Charcot, Jean-Martin 14
children
  attachment theory **54**
  discovering others 30
  identity formation 151
  infant development 30, **55**
  learning **48–49**, 53
  mental development **46–47**
  nature vs. nurture **13**
  psychological
    development **50–51**
choice theory **85**
Chomsky, Noam 58
Clark, Kenneth and Mamie 60
classical conditioning **32**
classification systems,
  psychiatric 107, **108–109**
cognitive behavioral therapy
  (CBT) 126, 134, **135**

cognitive behaviorism **37**
cognitive bias **103**
cognitive development 54,
  59
cognitive dissonance **97**
cognitive maps 36
cognitive psychology
  86–105, 94
collective unconscious **28**,
  129
commission, sins of **100–101**
commitment 71, 151
compulsions 118, 123
computational theory of
  mind **95**
concepts 47
conditioning
  behavioral **33**
  classical **32**
  law of effect **34**
  operant **35**
  social 31
conflict 50, **76**, 97
conformity 67
conscientiousness 143
conscious mind 22, 23, 24,
  129
consciousness 7, 87, **88–89**
  elements of **17**
  levels of **22–23**
  stream of 20
cooperation 41, 68, 76
creative intelligence/
  thinking 147, **148**
crystallized intelligence 146
Csikszentmihalyi, Mihaly 105
cultural naturalism **68**
culture 49, 62, 63, 68, 150,
  154–155
cyclothymia 113

D

Darley, John 77
Darwin, Charles 20, 68
decision-making 87, 95,
  102–103

defense mechanisms **25**
delusions 108, 112, 113,
  138
Democritus 11
dependent personality
  disorder **125**
depression 24, 94, 108, 113,
  114, 115, 138
Descartes, René 10
desires 12, 23
development, four stages of
  45, **47**
developmental psychology
  7, **44–65**
Dewey, John 68
difference, psychology of 7,
  140–155
disability 150
disgust 93
disorders, psychological 7,
  15, **106–139**
dissociative identity
  disorder (DID) 109, **121**
dreams 24, 28, 128
drives, primitive 23, 25
drug abuse 120, 123
dualism **10**, 11

E

eating disorders 109, **122**
Ebbinghaus, Hermann 19
education
  child-centered learning
  48
  Jigsaw Classrooms **61**
effect, law of **34**
egalitarianism 81
ego 22, 23, 25, 130
Ekman, Paul 93
Ellis, Albert 134
emotions 17, 94, 142, 143
  James–Lange theory of
  emotion 21
  psychology of **93**
environment 13, 45, 69,
  142, 152

Erikson, Erik 50–51, 150
Eros 23
ethnic identity development
  62
eugenics 146
Eurocentrism 84
evolutionary psychology **41**,
  68, 93
existential therapy 127, **133**
experience 9
  and knowledge **90–91**,
  103
  traumatic 24, 25
explicit memory 98
extroversion 143, **144**
eye movement
  desensitization and
  reprocessing (EMDR) 127,
  137

F

facial expressions 93
fairness 79, 83
familiarity 78
family systems therapy 127,
  136
fear 21, 93, 116, 117
femininity 63, 64
feminist psychology **152**
Festinger, Leon 97
field theory **69**
fight-or-flight response 116,
  120
fixed-action patterns **52**
flashbacks 120
flow **95**
fluid intelligence 146
focus **96**, 111
forgetting 100–101
  curve 19
free association 24, 128
Freud, Anna 25
Freud, Sigmund 12, 14,
  22–24, 28
Freudian slips 128
functionalism **20**

G

Galton, Francis 13
gambling 123
gender 64, 65, 70, 150
gender development **63**
generalized anxiety
    disorder (GAD) 109, **116**
genetics 13, 45, 52, **57**, 142
genograms 136
Gestalt psychology **18**
Gestalt therapy 127, **132**
Glasser, William 85
global workspace theory **89**
goals 95, 150, 151
Greenberg, Jerald 83

H

hallucinations 112, 113, 138
happiness **41**, 93
Harlow, Harry 55
Helmreich, Robert 81
heredity **13**
histrionic personality
    disorder **125**
heuristics **102**, 103
Hobbes, Thomas 11
hormones 42, 43
Horn, John 146
Horney, Karen 31
humanistic psychology 9, 127
hysteria **14**, 15

I

id 22, 23, 25
identity
    dissociative identity
        disorder **121**
    ethnic and racial **62**
    formation 51, **150**
    identity status theory **151**
implicit memory 98
imprinting 52
incompleteness, sense of 29

inferiority complex **26**
information processing 89,
    90–91, **94**
injustice 79, 83
instinctive behavior **52**
integrated information
    theory **89**
intelligence
    development of **47**
    theories of 141, **146–147**
interconnectedness 153
intimacy 71
introspection **16**, 17
introversion **144**

JKL

James, William 20, 21
Jigsaw Classrooms **61**
Jung, Carl 28, 129, 144
Jungian therapy 126, **129**
"just-world" hypothesis **79**
Kabat-Zinn, Jon 94
Kahneman, Daniel 102
Kinsey, Alfred 70
Klein, Melanie 30
knowledge
    acquired 146
    and perception **90–91**
    schemas **46**
Kohlberg, Lawrence 59
Kraepelin, Emil 15
Lacan, Jacques 29
Laing, R. D. 139
Lange, Carl 21
language 41, 49
    development 47, **58**
Latané, Bibb 77
latent learning **36**
learned behavior 34, 53
learned information **19**
learned response 32
Lerner, Max 79
Lewin, Kurt 69, 8
liberation psychology **84**
life space 69
limbic system 42

Loftus, Elizabeth 99, 100
logic 47, 102, 146
Lorenz, Konrad 52
love
    choice theory 85
    triangular theory of **71**

M

McClelland, David 149
Maccoby, Eleanor 64
McGregor, Douglas 82
Magical Number Seven **94**
management styles 82
mania 113, 138
MAOA gene 57
Marcia, James 151
marginalization 84
Martín-Baró, Ignacio 84
masculinity 63, 64
Maslow, Abraham 38, 39,
    40, 149
matter 11
medication 126, **138**
meditation **94**
memory 19, 41, 87, 95
    false **99**
    long-term 94, **98**
    pattern recognition **92**
    retrieving childhood 128
    seven sins of **100–101**
    short-term 94, 96, 98
    suppressed 24, 25
    working **94**
mere-exposure effect **78**
Milgram, Stanley 73
mind and body **10**
mindfulness **104**, 126
misattribution 99, 100
mood disorders 138
moral development **59**
mothers 30, 54, 55, 56
motivation **149**
multicultural psychology
    154–155
Myers, Linda James 153
myths 28

N

narcissistic personality
  disorder **125**
natural selection 41
nature
  interconnectedness 153
  vs. nurture **13**
needs
  choice theory **85**
  hierarchy of **38**
  need theory **149**
nervous system 7, **42–43**
neurons 42, 43
neuroscience 107
neurosis, layers of 132
neuroticism 143
neurotransmitters 42, 57, 138

O

obedience 67, **73**
object relations theory **30**
obsessive compulsive
  disorder (OCD) 109, 115,
  118
obsessive compulsive
  personality disorder **125**
OCEAN model **143**
omission, sins of **100–101**
openness 143
operant conditioning **35**
oppression **84**
optimal psychology **153**
organizational psychology
  82–83
others 30

P

panic disorders 109, 115,
  116, 117, 120
paranoid personality
  disorder **124**
passion 71
pattern recognition **92**

Pavlov, Ivan 32, 33
perception 17, 18, 87,
  90–91, 95, 132, 135
perinatal mental illness **115**
Perls, Fritz and Laura 132
person-centered therapy
  127, **131**
persona 129
personality
  and context **75**
  disorders 109, **124–125**
  and identity 150
  OCEAN model **143**
  testing 27, **145**
  trait theory 141, **142**
  type 27, 144
Phinney, Jean 62
phobias 109, **117**
physicalism **11**
Piaget, Jean 45, 46, 47, 48
Plato 10, 12
positive psychology **40**
posttraumatic stress
  disorder (PTSD) 109, **120**,
  138
power
  as motivator 149
  perception of **74**
practical intelligence 147
preconscious mind 22, 23
preference 78
pregnancy 115
prejudice 67, **80**
  racial 61
problem-solving 87
psychoanalysis **24**, 126, 128
psychoanalytic theory 9,
  22–23
psychodynamic therapy
  126, **128**
psychological development
  50–51
psychology, nature of **7**
psychometric tests **145**, 147
psychotic disorders 108,
  112–113, 115
punishment 35

R

race
  and identity 150
  Jigsaw Classrooms **61**
  racial identity
    development **62**
  and self-esteem **60**
rational emotive behavior
  therapy (REBT) 126, **134**
rationalization 25
Raynor, Rosalie 33
realistic conflict theory **76**
reality, aspects of human **29**
reason 12, 47
register theory **29**
reinforcement 35
relationships, family 136
religion 28, 150
repression 24, 25
responsibility
  avoidance of **77**
  for choices/actions 133
rituals 118
Rogers, Carl 39, 131
Rorschach, Hermann 27
Rorschach tests **27**, 145
rules of thumb **102**, 103

S

sadness 93
Schacter, Daniel 100
schemas **46**, 91
schizoid personality disorder
  124
schizophrenia 15, 108, **112**,
  138
schizotypal personality
  disorder **124**
scientific method 7, 9
security, sense of 54, 55, **56**
segregation, racial 60–61
self
  sense of 51, 88, 150
  true 129

self-acceptance 134
self-actualization **38**, 39
self-awareness 88, 132, 133
self-destructive behavior 29
self-esteem 26, 60, 114, 122
self-realization **31**
Seligman, Martin 40
sensations 17, 89
  processing **90–91**
sensorimotor stage 47
sex
  and autism **65**
  differences **64**
  gender identity **63**
  psychology of **70**
sexual abuse 57
shadow 129
Shapiro, Francine 137
Sherif, Muzafer 76
skills 95
Skinner, B. F. 35
social conditioning 31
social conformity **72**
social constructivism **49**
social context **75**
social injustice 84
social learning theory **53**
social phobia 117
social psychology 7, **66–85**, 141
socioeconomic status 150
soul, tripartite **12**
Spence, Janet T. 81
Stanford prison experiment **74**

stereotyping 61, 63, 64, 80
Sternberg, Robert 71, 147
stimuli 16, 21, 32, 33, 37, 52, 78, 145
Strange Situation, the **56**
stress 56, 109, 120, 136, 139
structuralism **17**, 18
suggestibility 99, 101
superego 22, 23, 25
surprise 93
symptoms, shared 15

T

talking therapies 126
testosterone 65
Thanatos 23
therapies **126–139**
Thorndike, Edward 34, 35
thoughts 17, 142
  challenging thought patterns **135**
  negative 94, 134, 135
Titchener, Edward 17
Tolman, Edward 36
top-down processing **91**
Torrance, Ellis Paul 148
Torrance Tests of Creative Thinking (TTCT) **148**
trait theory **142**
transactional analysis 126, **130**
transference 128
trauma 120, 121, 137
Treisman, Anne 96

trial and error 34
triarchic theory of intelligence **147**
trust 51, 131
Tversky, Amos 102

UVW

unconditional positive regard **39**, 131
unconscious, collective **28**, 129
unconscious mind 22, 23, 24, 25, 128, 145
values 133, 150
van Anders, Sari 70
Vygotsky, Lev 49
Watson, John 33
weight issues **122**
Weisstein, Naomi 152
Wing, Lorna 65
wisdom 50
women
  attitudes toward **81**
  feminist psychology **152**
  pregnancy/childbirth 115, 152
Wundt, Wilhelm 16, 17

Z

Zajonc, Robert 78
Zimbardo, Philip 74

ACKNOWLEDGMENTS

DK would like to thank the following for their help with this book: Phil Gamble, Daksheeta Pattni, and Vanessa Hamilton for the illustrations; Alexandra Beeden for proofreading; Helen Peters for the index; Mind's Lived Experience Leaders; Bethan Crisp, Alex Farines, Lewis Fewtrell, Julie Francis, Chloë Emily Fraser, Emma Harris, Dee Hudson, Amanda Joyce, Rebecca Myatt, Claire Simpson, Debs Smith, and Phoebe Stewart for authenticity reading; Senior Jacket Designer Suhita Dharamjit; Senior DTP Designer Harish Aggarwal; Senior Jackets Editorial Coordinator Priyanka Sharma.

All images © Dorling Kindersley
For further information see:
www.dkimages.com